William Joseph Buck

History of the Indian Walk, performed for the proprietaries of Pennsylvania in 1737, to which is appended a life of Edward Marshall

William Joseph Buck

History of the Indian Walk, performed for the proprietaries of Pennsylvania in 1737, to which is appended a life of Edward Marshall

ISBN/EAN: 9783337306182

Printed in Europe, USA, Canada, Australia, Japan

Cover: Foto ©ninafisch / pixelio.de

More available books at **www.hansebooks.com**

HISTORY

OF

THE INDIAN WALK

PERFORMED FOR THE

PROPRIETARIES OF PENNSYLVANIA IN 1737;

TO WHICH IS APPENDED A

LIFE OF EDWARD MARSHALL,

BY

WILLIAM J. BUCK,

MEMBER OF THE HISTORICAL SOCIETY OF PENNSYLVANIA;

Author of "History of Bucks County," "History of Moreland," "History of Montgomery County Within the Schuylkill Valley," "History of Montgomery County," "Life of Chief Justice Langhorne," "Contributions to the History of Bucks County," "The Cuttelossa," "The Local Historian," "Early Discovery of Coal in Pennsylvania," "Early Accounts of Petroleum in the United States," Etc.

PRINTED FOR THE AUTHOR.

1886.

Edition limited to Two Hundred and Ten Copies.

Entered according to Act of Congress, in the year 1886, by
WILLIAM J. BUCK,
In the Office of the Librarian of Congress at Washington.

PREFACE.

Of all that has been published relating to the history of Pennsylvania nothing probably has been more contradictory than that relating to the famous Indian Walk. Its beginning, general course and termination have more or less puzzled all writers who have attempted to treat upon it, without suspecting that it was on the part of the Proprietaries intentionally done to cover or conceal their proceedings. The date of its performance has also been a matter of speculation, owing to the conflicting character of the materials, without knowing until quite recently that there really had been a preliminary or trial Walk, which came thus to be confounded with the former though happening several years apart.

Since the publication of his history of Bucks county, in 1855, the writer has been a devoted collector of materials on this matter, but circumstances in a busy life have heretofore prevented their earlier preparation for the press. It was his fortune, however, to be employed by the Historical Society of Pennsylvania, to arrange the recently acquired Penn Papers from England, which occupied him more or less from October 1872, until 1876. While engaged in this labor pains were taken to secure extracts of whatever had a bearing on the subject. This enabled him afterwards to prosecute additional researches in the records of Philadelphia, Bucks and Northampton counties, and also to seek the descendants of Edward Marshall and others to help explain and make up deficiencies of what was most needed. As the collection was thus increasing, the many hundreds of items were classified under appropriate heads. These were next carefully compared and whatever was considered and believed to be the most reliable was made use of, giving contemporaneous documents the preference. While nothing of interest was omitted that appeared truthful a considerable amount, chiefly traditionary matter, had to be rejected, because so utterly at variance with original existing materials. Private correspondence of the period has been of great service in establishing facts and revealing the mysteries of the affair, showing that there was a design in keeping the matter concealed as far as possible from the public, and hence the cause of so many errors. No wonder the extensive Penn papers were so long withheld by the family until through their own dissensions they were hurried from out their possession and sold.

This may be well considered a labor of love. The long interval of one-third of a century has passed away since it was commenced. It was some incentive that on the line of the Walk the writer's ancestors have lived for several generations, and where also he was born, spent his early youth, and received his first traditions thereon. Not many miles away was also the Island home of Edward Marshall, which led to an acquaintance with a number of his descendants, whose assistance has since proved of great service as well as that of several others in the county, though now nearly all deceased. The information thus sought and obtained was fortunately noted down at the time and is now first made use of in this work. Authorities on all leading points have been carefully given in support of the writer's statements or where contrary views have been heretofore maintained.

In its beginning the Indian Walk appeared but a small affair that lay chiefly between the Proprietaries of Pennsylvania and the native Indians. With time the results of its injustice became more and more apparent and on the part of the Indians culminated in war and the most determined efforts for the recovery of their favorite hunting grounds of which they were defrauded by the extraordinary head-line drawn from the end of the Walk, costing the lives of hundreds of the unfortunate settlers. The Assembly of Pennsylvania, through their agent Dr. Franklin, had the affair laid before the King and Government of Great Britain for investigation, thus claiming attention on both sides of the Atlantic, and resulting in considerable feeling. However, the excitement attending it in Pennsylvania was preparing the people more and more for independence. The Indian Walk had a more important bearing on the history of Pennsylvania than has generally been supposed.

With these remarks the work is respectfully submitted to the judgment of candid and impartial readers.

W. J. B.

Jenkintown, Pa., September, 1886.

CONTENTS.

CHAPTER	PAGE
I.—The Proprietary Government,	7
II.—The Rights of the Indians,	20
III.—Lands Sold Not Granted by the Indians,	36
IV.—The Trial Walk,	53
V.—The Walking Purchase,	64
VI.—Preparations for the Walk,	82
VII.—The Indian Walk,	91
VIII.—Observations on the Walk,	99
IX.—Results of the Walk,	112
X.—What Brought Forth the Documents,	121
XI.—The Proprietaries and the Society of Friends,	137
XII.—Biographical Sketches of Prominent Persons Concerned in the Walk,	151

LIFE OF EDWARD MARSHALL.

CHAPTER	PAGE
I.—His Early Career,	203
II.—His Account of the Walk,	209
III.—Removes to Northampton County,	209
IV.—Indian Attacks on His Family,	222
V.—Bounties for Destroying Indians,	230
VI.—Returns to Bucks County,	239
VII.—Family Reminiscences and Traditions,	247
VIII.—Marshall's Island,	254
IX.—His Descendants,	259

THE INDIAN WALK.

CHAPTER I.

THE PROPRIETARY GOVERNMENT.

For a proper understanding of the Indian Walk, both as to its cause, effect and general results, a knowledge of the Proprietary government is necessary. During almost a century it exercised its powers over the destinies of what is now a great state, subject only to the King and Parliament of Great Britain. What that government was, its rights, duties and requirements, we propose to briefly investigate. Much has been written of what transpired during the colonial period, but not on this subject. Some had no desire to touch on it for the purpose of giving an expression of their views, and others again have so omitted it as to make it appear of small account, or only incidentally to show by its actions that there was such a power.

The Royal Charter was granted by King Charles II. to William Penn in 1681, as a reward for the merits and services of his father Admiral Penn, and to indulge his desire to enlarge the British Empire and civilize the savage natives. The form of government was to be proprietary; that is, the soil was given to him in fee, but he, his heirs and assigns and tenants, were to bear true faith and allegiance to the Crown. Penn and his successors were authorized to govern the country by a legislative body, to erect courts of justice and administer the laws, and generally do all things needful for the well-being of the inhabitants, so long as they kept within the statutes of the realm. An appeal to the tribunals of England was allowed, but in all cases the power there was to be regarded as final or conclusive. An agent was required to reside constantly in Great Britain to answer to alleged abuses, as for instance the acts of the Assembly here.

It will be seen from this that the proprietary government of Pennsylvania was nothing less than a hereditary monarchy invested in William Penn and his descendants, but at the same time dependent on Great Britain; the King being the source of all power, beyond whom there could be no appeal. In the third section of the Royal Charter is found the following feudal relic required in addition by the King from his liege subjects the Proprietaries: "paying thenceforth to us, our heirs and successors, two beaver skins, to be delivered at our Castle of Windsor, on the first day of January in every year; and also the fifth part of all gold and silver ore, which shall from time to time happen to be found within the limits aforesaid, clear of all charges." This tribute of two beaver skins was actually paid by the Penns from 1753 to 1780 we know, having seen the original receipts for the same.

By said charter the whole province was made the property of one man—that is, in a two-fold sense, of its soil and its government; and all this for the discharge of a debt, regardless of the rights of the Indians or of the people residing there. In the exercise of the legal power conferred on him Penn proceeded to frame a government and a code of laws of his own device, subsequently the cause of so much trouble. For one thing, however, he deserved credit, and that was for religious toleration; but from the force of circumstances, even had he been otherwise desirous, it could not have been well avoided, from the example set him some time before by the colonies of Rhode Island and Maryland.

Whenever the proprietaries were not disposed to come here and carry on the government themselves, they appointed by the right they possessed the deputy governors, who only held the office during their permission, and placed them under bonds of £5000 and approved security for their faithful performance and requisite loyalty, first due to the King and British government, next to the Proprietaries, and thirdly and, it might be added, lastly, to the province or colony.

This was a difficult task to assume, for there were three masters to serve, for what they owed to those abroad and what was due to the circumstances by which they were surrounded. It may be surprising that with all the power exercised over them yet the province paid their salaries, which were fixed and allowed by the Assembly.

There was a Council, which at first was elected every three years, consisting of eighteen persons and an Assembly, annually. The Council could only act with the advice of the Governor and with him possessed the appointing power. The powers of the Assembly extended little beyond making laws relating to the collecting and appropriating revenues.

The greatest power of the Penns to carry through any unjust designs against the will of the people or of the Assembly, who it appears were generally disposed to justice, lay in the appointing power. Thus the judges of the courts, the attorney general, surveyor general, and, if required, down to all their deputies, were appointed and commissioned by the governors and council through the instructions of the proprietaries, and should the governor disobey he would at once be set aside. The Council though in one sense independent was completely subordinate to the governor, without whom they could not act. Again, when duly obedient or passive, themselves and sons would likely at some time be rewarded by office or promotion. This was the general character of those in the courts as well as in other provincial offices. Likewise in the election of the various county officers by the people, the governor had still the right to appoint and commission either one of the two receiving the highest vote for the office. Thus in looking over our published Colonial Records and Archives, one will be struck at the appointing occasionally to office the one that received the next highest vote. This seems to have been most frequently exercised with regard to the sheriff's office, and which unfortunately was held only one year at a time. This information becomes important to explain in part how the Penns were enabled to plan, execute and carry out such an unjust act as the Walk on the Indians, and afterwards so successfully to smuggle away and conceal the public documents concerning the same that did not favor their interests.

The Penns being themselves almost continually involved in law suits in Great Britain, had acquired in this respect considerable experience, which knowledge they would turn to account in the government of Pennsylvania. Hence they kept a vigilant eye on those designed to be judges of the courts as well as sheriffs who had the selection of jurors. So much were those holding these positions their creatures, that in any case in which the interest of the Penns would be involved there could be but a poor chance for justice. It is doubtful whether in any of the other English colonies there could have been found so servile a set of judges and so devoted to the proprietary interest as those of Pennsylvania down to the Revolution. Thus in the collection of their quit rents and other revenues, the leasing and disposing of lands and in the disputes arising therefrom, they wielded a power that now can scarcely be credited. In those matters the royal government had no interest and was consequently indifferent, but it was otherwise with the people, who, as a general thing, were too liberty-loving to be blind to such gross abuses of power; and we need not wonder that there was such a spirit of opposition to the proprietaries, and that they preferred a government directly under the crown.

On the other hand the home government had its peculiar interests involved and to see after, about which the Penns were equally indifferent, yet which bore sorely on the province. The Assembly, as an instance, had here passed a law laying a duty on the importation of slaves and convicts from abroad. The following is a copy of instructions issued by command of the King to Governor George Thomas in regard to the same, dated the 10th of December, 1731 : " Whereas Acts have been passed in some of Our Plantations in America for laying Duties on the Importation and Exportation of Negroes, to the great Discouragement of the Merchants trading thither from the coast of Africa; and Whereas Acts have been likewise passed for laying of Duties on Felons imported in Direct opposition to an Act of Parliament passed in the fourth year of Our late Royal Father's Reign, for the further preventing Robbery, Burglary and other Felonies, and for the more effectual Transportation of Felons—it is our Will and Pleasure, that you do not give your Assent to or pass any Law imposing Duties upon Negroes into Our Province of Pennsylvania payable by the importer, or upon any slaves exported, that have not been sold in Our said Province and continued there for the space of Twelve Months. It is our further Will and Pleasure, that you do not give your Assent to or pass any Act whatever for imposing Duties on the Importation of any Felons from this Kingdom into Our said Province of Pennsylvania."

The first Charter of Privileges for the province was made in England April 25, 1682, and the second, April 2, 1683. These were set aside by Penn for a new one he framed, signed October 28, 1701, and which continued in force till into the Revolution, when, of course, it was supplanted by a state constitution. On this last it becomes us now to touch, for compared to the previous ones as respects privileges the people were made considerably the losers while the proprietary powers were greatly strengthened. The Council, or what we might call the Senate, were no longer elective; the Proprietary had now assumed the sole right to select and dismiss them at his pleasure. In the third article of this charter (see the whole in Colonial Records, Vol. II, pp. 56–61) we find "That the freemen in each respective county, at the time and place of meeting for electing their representatives to serve in Assembly, may, as often as there shall be occasion, choose a double number of persons to present to the governor, sheriffs and coroners, if so long they behave themselves well, out of which respective elections and presentments the governors shall nominate and commissionate one for each of the said offices." Though elections were held and appeared free, yet with such restrictions they could amount to little but to render officials extremely pliant and tractable to the measures or designs of the proprietaries. We need not wonder at the high-handed or arbitrary proceedings of such men as deputy governors Evans and Denny, backed as they were by the powers to which they owed and held their positions.

Gordon in his History of Pennsylvania (pp. 121–3) mentions another strong point gained by the Proprietary in the new charter. "Nor was the Council recognized as a part of the government, unless a prohibition to the Governor and Council to take cognizance of any complaint relating to property, except appeals should be allowed by law from the ordinary tribunals, may be considered as such recognition. The practice of trying causes relative to real estate, before the Governor and Council, as well as those in which private citizens were parties, as those in which the Proprietary was interested, had been continued. This made him a judge in his own cause, and was highly objectionable when the Council was elected by the people; it became wholly admissible when that body became the mere creature of the Governor."

Just before his final departure, Penn appointed ten persons for the Council, of whom four were to be a quorum. Respecting these he says, "to continue in place till my further order shall be known: and I further hereby grant to my Lieutenant Governor for the time being full power and authority upon the decease or removal of any of the said Council, to nominate and appoint others to serve in their place and stead, also to add to the number of the Council now appointed." So passed away the independent elective Council, and other extensive powers of the people.

Ellis in his Life of Penn (p. 372) is therefore considerably mistaken when he says that "the new frame of Government was essentially the same, except in allowing the territories to separate from the government of the Province". Janney still more absurdly remarks (Life of Penn, second edition, p. 451) that "in some respects was even more liberal than those which preceded it." Penn signed at New Castle, October 31, 1701, the charter for the borough of Chester, wherein he styles himself, perhaps for the first time, "true and absolute Proprietary and Governor-in-Chief of the Province of Pennsylvania, and Territories thereunto belonging."

Coming down to a later period, the Indian war of 1754 broke out, one of the causes of which was attributed to the unfairness of the Walk, and the advantage taken therefrom by the Proprietaries to defraud them of a great quantity of land, and even selling it to speculators some time previous to their legal ownership of the same. The war thus brought about involved considerable expense and bore rather heavily on the colony. With a view of equalizing taxation, the Assembly passed a bill levying £100,000 upon all estates, real and personal, including alike, and for the first time, that of the Proprietaries. Governor Denny, as their deputy, rejected it, and, however unjustly, the people were forced to submit to the exemption. But the Assembly determined to send two commissioners to England, to present their grievances before the throne, and obtain relief. Isaac Norris and Benjamin

Franklin were selected for this purpose; but the former, on account of ill health and his private affairs, did not accept, and the latter proceeded alone, arriving in London in July, 1757, and laid his instructions before the government. This at once raised the ire of the Penns, and involved considerable controversy. However, in 1759, a final decision was given on this vexed question, favoring the province, which was looked upon as a signal triumph by Franklin and his party.

From the "Heads of Complaint," presented by Franklin as agent, August 20, 1757, we give the following extracts: "That the reasonable and necessary power given to Deputy Governors of Pennsylvania by the Royal Charter, sections 4th and 5th, of making Laws with the Advice and Consent of the Assembly for raising Money for the Safety of the Country and other public uses according to their best discretion, is taken away by Proprietary Instructions enforced by penal Bonds, and restraining the Deputy from the use of his best discretion, tho being on the spot, he can better judge of the emergency, state and necessity of affairs, than the Proprietaries residing at a great distance. That the indubitable right of the Assembly to judge of the Mode, Measure and time of Granting supplies, is infringed by Instructions that enjoin the Deputy to refuse his assent to any Bill for raising money, unless certain Modes, Measures and Times in such Instructions directed, make a part of the Bill whereby the Assembly in time of war are reduced to the necessity of either losing the country to the

Enemy, or giving up the Liberties of the People and receiving Law from the Proprietary. That the Proprietaries have enjoined their Deputy by secret instructions to refuse his assent to any law for raising money by a Tax though ever so necessary for the Defence of the country, unless the greatest part of their estate is exempted from such tax. This to the Assembly and people of Pennsylvania appears both unjust and cruel. The Proprietaries are now requested seriously to consider these complaints and redress the aggrievances complained of in the most speedy and effectual Manner, that Harmony may be restored between the several Branches of the Legislature and the Public service be hereafter readily and fully provided for."

Sherman Day, in his able work on Pennsylvania, speaking of the troubles existing at this time, truthfully remarks: "On the one side was the proprietary family, with their feudal prerogatives, their manors of 10,000 acres, their quit-rents, and baronial pomp, —alienated in their sympathies from the colony— preferring the luxuries of aristocratic life in England, to the unostentatious manners of the new world—ruling the colonies by capricious deputies—and ever refusing to be taxed for the common defence of the country. On the other side was a hardy and enthusiastic band of colonists, free in this new world to develop the great principles of civil liberty, then just dawning upon the human mind—willing to bear their share provided the proprietaries would consent to be equally taxed."

In a letter from Thomas Penn, dated July 1, 1755, to Isaac Norris, we take the following extract, from which it appears he was not by any means ignorant of the feeling engendered against himself and several of the family: "I am greatly concerned to find such a spirit of discontent gone forth in Pennsylvania, against us and our government, as I think we have not given any just cause for it. However, I hope the people themselves will soon be convinced they have been most grossly imposed upon."

"In Franklin's day," remarks his biographer, James Parton, "the Proprietaries were two in number, Thomas Penn, who owned three-fourths of the province, and Richard Penn, who owned one-fourth. Thomas Penn was a man of business—careful, saving and methodical. Richard Penn was a spendthrift. Both were men of slender abilities, and not of very estimable character. But, unhappily, they cherished those erroneous tory notions of the rights of sovereignity which Lord Bute infused into the contracted mind of George III., and which cost that dull and obstinate monarch his colonies. These Penns, in addition to the pride of possessing acres by the million, felt themselves to be lords of the land they owned, and of the people who dwelt upon it. And it must be confessed, they were long upheld in this belief by the Pennsylvanians themselves. When one of the Proprietaries deigned to visit the province, he received the address, as a king might from his subjects, and replied to them with a brevity more than royal. The tone and style of all their later communications to the Pennsylvanians was that of offended lords to countenanced vassals. And yet, at home, as William Franklin wrathfully records, they were so insignificant as 'hardly to be found in the herd of gentry; not in court, not in office, and not in parliament.' "

CHAPTER II.

THE RIGHTS OF THE INDIANS.

We now come to the subject of what were the recognized rights of the Indians to the soil under the royal charter, and by the proprietaries, and what obligations the latter were under to observe justice towards them in taking their lands or disposing of them to others. It appears that the Dutch, from the earliest occupation of both sides of the Delaware, recognized a right in the Indians to the soil, by the repeated purchases made from them, up even to the mouth of the Schuylkill, previous to 1648. In the instructions from Queen Christina, of Sweden, in 1643, to Governor John Printz, he was particularly directed, in his dealings with the Indians, to confirm the former purchases of lands and treaties of peace, and as far as practicable to win them over to embrace christianity and adopt the manners and customs of civilized life. The Rev. John Campanius, Chaplain of the Colony from 1642 to 1648, was so encouraged by the kindness and docility of the natives, that he learned their language and translated Luther's catechism into it, of which Charles XI., in 1696, had 500 copies printed and sent over here to be distributed by his countrymen among the Indians with a view to their religious instruction and mental improvement, though now for fourteen years the colony of Penn. We find a similar act of kindness exhibited by the small band of Moravians who first settled in 1740 within the present limits of Northampton county, and who through the long and devoted labors of that pious missionary, David Zeisberger, established schools among them with spelling books and other works in their language, to advance their moral and intellectual condition. As we have examined the works of these Swedish and German missionaries, and reflected on the sway here of the Penns for nearly a century, the question would naturally arise, what acts of disinterested benevolence towards them did they or even the kings of England exhibit?

It was the fortune of William Penn in the formation of his colony to have dealings with the gentlest natives, and endowed with the noblest traits of all those found inhabiting the eastern portion of the present United States. The many acts of kindness exhibited to the early Swedish, English and German settlers of Pennsylvania, and transmitted by them to us, if collected, would readily fill a volume; nay, the writings of William Penn himself bear evidence of this, and are quite full on the subject. In corroboration of what has been said of the Delawares, we have also the high authority of General William H. Harrison, expressed as late as the beginning of this century, when it is likely that they may have become more corrupted by intercourse with the whites. "A long and intimate knowledge of them, in peace and war, as enemies and friends, has left upon my mind the most favorable impressions of their character for bravery, and fidelity to their engagements."

Among the papers of Thomas Penn was found a printed broadside, without date, but evidently before 1750; and we have reason to believe, published as instructions by order of the British government to the several proprietaries and governors, and from the nature of its injunctions kept confidential. The following is an extract: "From September, 1745, to the present time His Majesty's province of New Jersey is in open Rebellion; and unless some speedy and effectual measures are soon taken, his Majesty's government, Laws and Authority, not only in this, but in the neighboring Provinces, whose inhabitants, for the most part, are but too well inclined to receive the infection, will in all probability be absolutely destroyed. The pretense for the Rebellion on foot is, that the Right to the soil of that Province is in the native Indians, and Persons claiming under them, and not in the Crown or its Grantees, and that no title is good but that from the Indians; thus unhinging all Property there, denying the rights and prerogatives of the Crown, and setting up the Indian's Right in opposition thereto."

An examination of the royal charter shows nothing in it recognizing any right or title of the Indians whatever to the soil, or that they possessed any other claims. Next we went over the "Frame of Government" prepared by Penn in 1682, and also the charters of 1686 and 1696; but with no more satisfaction. Again, in Smith's Laws of Pennsylvania, published in Philadelphia in 1810 (Vol. 11, p. 137), is an able article on Indian titles, from which the following extract is taken: "By force of the royal charter, William Penn, and his successors as proprietaries were the undoubted lords of the soil. They stipulated, however, with the purchasers under them to extinguish the right of the natives. They alone had this power. No individual, without their authority, could purchase of the Indians; and the people themselves, by legislative acts, recognized and aided them to enforce this important principle." We readily admit the truth of the aforesaid, with but a single exception, that "They," the said proprietaries, "*stipulated* with the purchasers under them to extinguish the right of the natives." These stipulations we should like to see, as to their nature, and whether they were so worded as to show an intent to deal fairly and honorably.

In respect to this we have the opinions of some of the most intelligent people in the colony at the very time that William Penn was with us, who publicly charged him with his conduct though members of the same religious denomination. Turning to the appendix of Proud's History of Pennsylvania (Vol. 11, p. 40), we find an address drawn up by the Assembly and signed by Joseph Growdon, Speaker, and delivered September 20, 1701, in contemplation of his speedy departure. Disposed to be brief, we shall only take a short extract from it: "May it please the Governor. That before the Proprietary go to *England*, he grant us such an instrument as may absolutely secure and defend us in our estates and properties, from himself, his heirs and assigns, for ever, any claiming under, him, them, or any of them, as also to clear all *Indian purchases* and others." Though a reply was made to the address, no notice whatever of the aforesaid petition, however just and reasonable, was taken, and so the Governor left it to his posterity, and they in turn, as we shall see, did not improve upon it. The members composing that Assembly nearly all belonged to the Society of Friends. They were good men and peaceably disposed, and would not have thus pressed on him a deferred matter at the very last opportunity, if they had not known injustice had been done the Indians, which, if not checked in time, must end in open hostilities, and in consequence looked to the future with serious apprehensions.

Without peace, Penn well knew that his interests must suffer, and seriously interfere in the disposal of lands to actual settlers and the peopling of his colony. He knew the power he possessed and he meant to keep it, and consequently would purchase *in his own way and manner*, as best suited him. It was a market in which he alone could buy if he desired, and in which there could even be no interference. This will account for the vagueness of the deeds of purchase and the trivial nature of many of the articles paid, which some in their ignorance have gone so far as to call *presents*, as if no consideration had been given. Further, he could not well shirk the examples set by the repeated purchases made by the Dutch, Swedes and English before him, in now his own territory; as in the case of Governor Andros, of New York, in 1679, of no inconsiderable tract along the Delaware within the limits of the present Bucks county.

There is no evidence that we know of before Penn's day of any dissatisfaction here on the part of the Indians on this subject; in proof they were easy to deal with and entertained every confidence. His correspondence during his residence here contains numerous aspersions of the character and dishonesty of those with whom he had dealings. An opinion of the man both in this and in many other respects may be formed from reading his correspondence with James Logan, lately published by the Historical Society in two volumes. This is also exhibited in his establishing "Courts of Inquiry" the 10th of December, 1700, in the several counties, and appointing three judges to each with the intent of "examining, searching and inquiring into the rights, titles and claims of all freeholders," and to make them produce their titles or claims to the same, and "also carefully to enquire into all escheats, fines and forfeitures" that are fallen to him and also of his quit-rents. To carry this into execution they were empowered to call to their aid "all needful officers, especially ye Constables." But where was the power to similarly enquire as to his dealings with the Indians?

By the deed of July 15, 1682, a purchase was made by his agent and cousin, William Markham, from the mouth of the Neshaminy up the Delaware to a corner spruce tree standing on the river's bank "about Makeerickkitton and from thence running along the ledge or foot of the Mountains, West North West to a corner White Oak marked with the letter P, standing by the Indian Path that leadeth to an Indian Town called Playwicky, and from thence extending Westward to the Neshaminy Creek." This boundary or limit is copied from a paper furnished by the Penns and consequently should appear to be to their satisfaction. In vain, it would seem, have all efforts been made ever since by disinterested persons to satisfactorily establish this line. Where it should really be we will not take upon us to say, but Benjamin Eastburn, the surveyor general and agent for the proprietaries, established it fifty-five years later evidently to his satisfaction and to that of his employers. This map, prepared expressly for Thomas Penn, and long in his possession and closely kept, has at last found its way back here again, and we have kindly been permitted to examine and copy it. To the surprise, we know, of many in that vicinity, this boundary is placed at or very near Hough's creek on the Delaware, thence by the Newtown and Wrightstown township line to the Neshaminy. Comparing Thomas Holmes' Map of original purchasers with Eastburn's Map, confirms this opinion the more. Whatever views may be entertained or expressed hereafter as to the locality, we shall assume this as the proper line, and in consequence see here the cause for an early expression of dissatisfaction on the part of the Indians.

John Chapman, in 1684, purchased a tract of upwards of five hundred acres, located on the north side of said line, and on which he settled with his family. Though this land was here laid out to him, no satisfaction whatever had been made to the Indians for it, as well as that sold to all others settling in what are now the present townships of Wrightstown, Upper Makefield, Buckingham, Solebury and several others situated northwards. Samuel Smith, in his History of the Province of Pennsylvania (see Hazard's Register, Vol. 1, p. 215), in speaking of Chapman's early settlement, goes on to say: "The Indians were now numerous hereabouts, and used to frequent Chapman's house in great companies as they had occasion to pass that way, but behaved themselves civilly. One of the Chiefs, however, one day coming to him, in an angry tone told him it was their land he was settled on, pointing to a small distance, where he said the bounds of the English purchase were, and borrowing an axe, marked a line to the southeast of his house, and went away without giving him any further trouble at that time." The chief aforesaid may possibly have been Idquahon, also called Nicholas, a son of Tamany, and one of the signers to the deeds of July 15, 1682, and of July 15, 1694, and would therefore be likely to have a knowledge of the true boundary, which agrees with that on Eastburn's map. In the Colonial Records (Vol. I, p.

396), we have additional information about him. At a Council held in Philadelphia December 19, 1693: "The informant, Polycarpus Rose, saith, that about five weeks since, having some discourse with a certain Indian King called Hicquoqueen, the said Indian resented the unkindness of the English to the Indians here, and further said, that they were not like to hold the Land much longer; for that they were not satisfied for it."

No satisfactory authority has yet been produced, that north from said line of Newtown township to the Delaware, and up along said river to the south side of the Lehigh hills above Durham, and thence westward, any purchase *had ever been made of the Indians* previous to the deed of September 17, 1718. Yet in the interval of 1682 to the aforesaid date, considerable of this land had been sold to speculators and actual settlers, by order of the Proprietary, William Penn, or his family, through their agents. This, it should be remembered, was done while he was living; for he died July 30, 1718, only forty-eight days before the completion of that purchase. That the Indians did not bear this very well we have further evidence. John Streiper, a native and resident of the Duchy of Juliers, on the borders of Germany, in 1683, purchased of William Penn 5000 acres of land, which was located by the commissioners of property, and surveyed and laid off to him March 26, 1701, between the Tohickon creek and Delaware river, now in Tinicum township. Said tract was further confirmed to him under the great seal of the Province, June 24, 1705. Now, the said John Streiper, also his attorney, and after his death in 1717, his heirs, tried in various ways to sell it, but in vain, alleging that all their endeavors "*had no effect, because of a claim made to the land by the Indians, who say they never yet sold it.*" This matter, sorely against their wishes and earnest remonstrances, lingered till 1725, when it was, through the hands of James Logan, returned to the heirs of William Penn. We have in this a strong instance of a powerful, virtuous sentiment prevailing here among the mass of the people, not only in respecting their own rights but the rights of others.

In making researches in the Bucks county records, a deed was found given by William Penn the 17th of 11th month, 1701 (see Deed Book 6, p. 275), for £100, to George Beale, of Surry, England, for 3000 acres of land " to be clear of *Indian Incumbrances*, in said province, between the rivers of Susquehanna and Delaware." This is the only instance in our knowledge of any stipulation whatever from Penn respecting the Indian title. His vexatious and numerous lawsuits, pecuniary embarrassments, increasing debts and extravagant children, may have brought him to this issue, with a purchaser whose will was fully as strong as his own when the choice was presented of no sale or such conditions.

The relations existing between the Penns and the colonists were unfortunate. By their actions the former exhibited, beyond their own interests, but little regard for the rights of either the Indians or the people. Coming here on occasional visits, when it suited them, and with attachments so strong for the old world that even the bodies of those of the family dying were sent back for interment, we need not wonder that the people cared as little for them, and were made still worse by their own profligate conduct. The royal charter sets forth that it is to indulge the desires of William Penn in enlarging the bounds of the British Empire and to civilize the savage natives there, as among the reasons for giving him the grant. It might now well be asked: What was even attempted in the way of civilizing the Indians? Yet it would appear as one of the reasons pleaded by him in his petition to the King.

As a sneer at christianity, Voltaire said, nearly a century after the occurrence, that Penn's great treaty with the Indians had been the first not ratified by an oath and never broken. Such a random conjecture, however eloquent it may sound, scarcely merits a reply. To know whether it was not broken, if there really was such a one, even shortly after it was made, *we must possess the evidence on what it was founded and the obligations there entered into by the contracting parties.* That there has never been anything of the kind since produced to either justify or establish such claims, is well known. As other documents have been abstracted, forbidden inspection, and missing, in relation to certain interests, why may not this too explain in part the mysteries that have ever since invested the great treaty, and about which so much has been said and little or nothing known? The charges and apprehensions of the Assembly on this subject, so publicly expressed, and to which Penn did not deign even an allusion, and the selling of lands to speculators and actual settlers without regard to the claims of the Indians being first satisfied, is too strong for an impartial historian to pass by or to justify.

Respecting the merits of William Penn in his dealings with the Indians, Peter Du Ponceau and J. Francis Fisher, in "A Memoir on the Celebrated Treaty" (see Memoirs of Hist. Soc. Penn., Vol. III, p. 192), make these sensible remarks: "We must observe in the first place that it is not on this treaty that depends the fame of our illustrious founder, nor is it on his having purchased his lands of the Indians; instead of taking them by force. Others before him, had made treaties of friendship and of alliance with the original possessors of the American soil; others had obtained their lands from them by fair purchase; in Pennsylvania the Swedes, the Dutch and the English, who governed the country during the space of eighteen years under the Duke of York, had pursued the same peaceable system; it is, therefore, not only unjust, but it is extremely injudicious, to endeavor to ascribe to William Penn the exclusive merit of a conduct pointed out, not only by the plainest rules of justice and the example of his predecessors, but also by prudence and the soundest policy, particularly when it is considered how much easier and cheaper it was to purchase the lands of these savage tribes than to attempt to take them by force, which in the infancy of colonies would not have been an easy task."

James Logan, in a letter to James Steel, dated Philadelphia, November 18, 1729, remarks : " Save it is now not only Sassoonan our very good friend and his people of our own Indians that we have to deal with but the lands also on Delaware above Tohickon creek must be purchased of others. But the main business of all is to induce John Penn himself to come over. The Indians all expect him next spring, every body expects him and it is in vain for him to expect that others will do his business for him." Here is a candid admission from one who had been so long Penn's secretary that, even down to 1729, the Indians had not been treated with, or paid, for lands above Tohicon, and for which they have always contended, yet considerable tracts had there for sometime previously been sold.

A petition dated 13th of 9th month, 1731, was sent to John, Thomas and Richard Penn, by Isaac Norris, Samuel Preston and James Logan, wherein they say : " We have divers times jointly, but we suppose James Logan oftener, represented to you the state of this Province and the necessity there appeared that one of you should hasten over as well to settle your affairs of Property as to enter on Treaties and to take measures with the native Indians for continuing that peace and good understanding with them, and these representations we hoped would have had the desired effect.

But your coming being from time to time deferred we thought it proper that James Steel, now two years ago, should take a voyage over in order more earnestly to press and if possible prevail with you to resolve on it without more delay, and on the account he gave us at his return we fully depended on seeing Thomas the same fall, but with the following spring and another fall are all passed away without now giving us much more hopes of what has been so long expected as three or four years ago. But a treaty we must have with them if possible if we would expect to continue in any manner of safety." What evidences we see herein of dissatisfaction on the part of the Indians through the continued neglect or indifference of the Penns, thus promoting with the increase of population the encroachments of the whites and inciting the Indians to hostilities in self defence.

The Delaware Indians, having become independent of the Six Nations, induced Thomas and Richard Penn as proprietaries to issue to them a most flattering "Address" from London February 28, 1759, from which we give an extract in contrast with the aforesaid: "To our Friends and Brethren the Indians of the Delaware Nation. We assure you since you have chose to lay this matter before the King we will answer it as speedily as possible and do every thing to shew you and all the World our desire to act a fair honest and kind part by you, and do expect when you shall be satisfied that we have not been guilty of so base an act as to forge or alter a Deed, that you will openly and plainly declare such your belief. As you are now restored by the consent of the Six Nations to the power of holding Treaties, we shall always confer with you with great pleasure." The principal aim of this was, of course, for affect among the colonists here, to mollify censure.

As a result of the complaints of the Delaware Indians before Sir William Johnson at Easton in June, 1762, a Royal Proclamation from George III. was issued dated October 7, 1763, which was required by order of the Lords Commissioners of Trade and Plantations to be published by Gov. John Penn. From this we take an extract seeming to reflect on the conduct of the proprietaries: "And whereas great Frauds and Abuses have been committed in the purchasing Lands of the Indians; in order therefore to prevent such irregularities for the future and to the end that the Indians may be convinced of our justice, and determined Resolution to remove all reasonable Cause of Discontent, We do, with the Advice of our Privy Council, strictly enjoin and require, that no private person do presume to make any Purchase from the said Indians of any lands reserved to the said Indians within those Parts of our Colonies where we have thought proper to allow settlement; but that if, at any Time, any of the said Indians should be inclined to dispose of the said Lands, the same shall be purchased only for us, in Our Name, at some public Meeting or Assembly of the said Indians, to be held for that purpose by the Governor or Commander-in-Chief of our

THE RIGHTS OF THE INDIANS.

Colonies respectively, within which they shall lie; and in case they shall lie within the limits of any Proprietaries, conformable to such Directions and Instructions as we or they shall think proper to give for that purpose." Here is seen, probably for the first time, some acknowledgment on the part of the Royal Government that the Indians did possess some right to the soil. But it came rather too late for justice and good faith to the few dwindling natives who had survived the Walk of more than a quarter of a century before, with the exterminating wars waged almost continuously against them from 1754 to the date of this proclamation.

CHAPTER III.

LANDS SOLD NOT GRANTED BY THE INDIANS.

As has been stated, all lands located and sold by the proprietary or his agents between the years 1682 and 1718, north of the Newtown township line and Hough's creek, thence extending up the Delaware river to the south side of the Lehigh hills and for some distance westward, were so disposed of without any title from the Indians and, as we may well suppose, without their knowledge or consent. No satisfactory evidence has yet been produced to the contrary in the long lapse of time passed away, and we now come to show that this unjust practice was knowingly continued by the sons of William Penn.

From the foot of the hills below the Lehigh and extending up along the Delaware to the extreme northern line of Pennsylvania, and thence westward from said river to the limits of the province, there is no proof by any deeds on record or any other conveyances, that previous to the satisfactory adjustment of the Walk of September 19 and 20, 1737, based on the deed of August 25th preceding, any Indian title or claim whatever had been extinguished to even a portion of this territory in all of said interval. Yet with the same recklessness or disregard for consequences the Penns continued selling to speculators and actual settlers as it best suited them. There is something remarkable about the deed of July 30, 1718—that the proprietaries should in no way make any reference to it in their subsequent dealings with the Indians.

James Logan, so long the secretary of William Penn, principal commissioner of lands, and agent of Indian affairs, demands our first attention. These offices we believe Logan held till on or near the close of his life in 1751. Turning to Smith's Laws of Pennsylvania (Vol. II., p. 113), the following information will be found respecting Indian complaints, with this gentleman's reply: "When the natives sold their lands, it was understood distinctly, that the white people should not settle or encroach upon their hunting grounds, and the lands reserved by them; nor was a single attempt thus to settle, unattended by complaints and uneasiness. The Indians observed their treaties with fidelity, and the boundaries appear to have been always accurately understood by them. The settlers notwithstanding encroached on the Indian lands beyond this boundary which occasioned great anxiety and uneasiness among the Delawares. The complaints of the aged Sassoonan were eloquent and pathetic."

At the treaty at Philadelphia, in 1728, Sassoonan, addressing himself to James Logan, said "That he was grown old, and was troubled to see the Christians settle on lands that the Indians had never been paid for; they had settled on his lands, for which he had never received anything; that he was now an old man, and must soon die; that his children may wonder to see all their father's lands gone from them without his receiving any thing for them; that the Christians made their settlements very near them, and they would have no place of their own left to live on; that this might occasion a difference between their children hereafter, and he would willingly prevent any misunderstanding that might happen." Mr. Logan, with the leave of the Governor, answered that "William Penn had made it a rule, never to suffer any lands to be settled by his people, till they were first purchased of the Indians; that his commissioners had followed the same rule." Now for a test as to said reply and that he did knowingly purchase and deal in such lands not only for himself but for others.

On the 29th of December, 1702, Mr. Logan purchased of the Commissioners of Property, Edward Shippen, Griffith Owen and *himself*, five hundred acres, at the Great Spring, in Solebury township, Bucks county, and which he some time afterwards by will donated to the Philadelphia Library. As one of the said commissioners he sold considerable more to others in that section and further north; for instance, the same year five hundred and eighty acres to William Beeks, and in 1703 twenty-five hundred acres to John White, near the present Lumberville. We believe he was also one of the same who sold in 1701 to John Streiper five thousand acres above the mouth of the Tohickon, and ten thousand acres November 16, 1727, to William Penn, Jr., located between the mouth of the Lehigh and Lackawaxen. Here are certainly strong and grave charges, and they show complicity with the proprietaries through his official relations.

In a tolerably lengthy report of a committee of Assembly to Sir William Johnson, dated Easton, June 22, 1762, and signed by John Hughes, Joseph Galloway, Edward Pennington, John Morton, Joseph Fox, Samuel Rhoads, Giles Knight and Isaac Pearson, we believe nearly all Friends, his conduct is further exposed. "To confirm," they say, "what we have already offered, we also lay before you a copy of a letter, compared with the original now in our hands, wrote by James Logan, Esquire, formerly President of the Council of this Province, secretary to the Governor and near forty years Commissioner of Property under the Proprietaries, directed to Thomas Watson, declaring that the lands four miles above on the Lehigh Mountains and to the south of the Forks of the Delaware were not on the 20th of November, 1727, nine years after the deed of 1718, and forty-one years after the Deed of 1686, purchased from the Indians; and therefore forbade the said Watson who was then the Proprietary Surveyor for Bucks county, to survey the same for one Joseph Wheeler."

If he was "near forty years commissioner of property," as is stated, and which we do not question, he must have been instrumental in knowingly selling in said time many thousands of acres of such lands, besides what he may have bought himself. We have also proof in the case of John Streiper, even some time before 1717, about the Indian complaints at Tohickon, that none of this land had in any way been cleared from their claims. To rebut in any way the aforesaid and what follows can only be done by records of the time, that all of said tracts had been first previously honorably purchased and paid for to the full satisfaction of the Indians. Of course the due recording and preserving of such contracts lay with the proprietaries, who alone had the power and whose interest it was. Of his eldest son, William Logan, however, we shall have good words. He was awhile at first in the Governor's council, but shortly after the death of his father and a further acquaintance with the conduct of Thomas Penn to the Indians, he openly opposed him, and the result was a sharp correspondence on the subject; but it sealed his fate in the future as to any favors from that source.

That James Logan was not ignorant of the complaints of the Indians and how far he was a party in the disposal of their lands will be further revealed in the following extracts taken from his correspondence. On the 20th of Ninth-month, 1727, he wrote to Jacob Taylor, the Surveyor General: "I have directed our overseer Wm. Foy at Durham to supply you therewith whatsoever you may want that they may have, and particularly to deliver you four of the best strowds blue and red for the present. It will require some caution in managing the survey which yet ought to be effectually done to prevent uneasiness to the Indians, but you will want no advice on that head. I heartily wish you success and a safe return." Five days later he wrote to John Penn in England: "There is not above two or three thousand acres of that rich land and the adjoining is all rocks and hills, yet it is not above sixty miles or thereabouts from Hudson's river. The Dutch people of New York government set a very great value upon it and were it clear of Indian claims would sell for good pay and at a high rate, perhaps 60 or 70£ per 100 acres if not more. Those bottoms, I mean, for the rest is good for nothing. I wish we may get the survey completed without any opposition from the Indians for which I have taken all possible precautions and these lands will be William's." On December 6th following, Logan wrote again: "Late last night Jacob Taylor and company returned from their journey up the river to lay out those low lands on Delaware to thy nephew William, in which they had no other success than with a present to the Indians of about 6£ value. The Indians would suffer no manner of survey to be made there on any account whatsoever. There never was any pretence of a purchase made on thy Father's account within thirty miles of the nearest of these Indian settlements."

In regard to planning the Walk and in making the most of it, few could be more pecuniarily interested than William Allen, and in this respect he is placed next only to Thomas Penn, who was the head and power behind the throne. Though a native of Philadelphia, for a long time through his wealth and position he wielded a great influence. No man in the province was more devoted, right or wrong, to the interests of the Penns; it was in fact the leading motive of his life. The result was the reward of great favors and official position. To show further his intimate relations with the family, Governor John Penn, the grandson of the founder and the offerer of rewards for Indian scalps, was married to his daughter Ann. His wife was Margaret, the sister of Governor James Hamilton, who also owed his elevation to the same source. These matters are all essential to a knowledge of what in modern parlance are called "ring movements." Mr. Allen figures so much from the very beginning of the Walk to its close, that for the present we will only dwell superficially on his immense dealings in lands *unpurchased from the Indians*. Could the whole be brought together and investigated, the result of his operations would be astonishing and would show an amount of injustice scarcely to be imagined.

William Penn, the founder, by will granted to his grandson, William Penn, Jr., ten thousand acres, which the latter sold to Mr. Allen, August 29, 1728. As soon as selected it was laid out by warrant to Jacob Taylor, the surveyor general, dated November 16, 1727. Perhaps the first thus taken up inside of a year from this date, was part of a larger tract, but we know by the Bucks county records (see Deed Book, No. 6, pp. 86,87), that this portion comprised over three-hundred acres in the Minisink region, some distance above the Water Gap. This was sold September 10, 1733, to Nicholas Depue. The information in this grant is very important, for just such proceedings have involved civilized nations of latter times in war, and no doubt was one of the causes that led not long afterwards to such savage attacks on the devoted settlers by the exasperated Indians, who had been deprived of their favorite hunting grounds. First is mentioned an "Island situate in the river Delaware, commonly called Mawwallamink, lying opposite to the Plantation where the said Nicholas Depue now dwels and contains 126 acres. The second Island called the Great Shawna Island, is situated in the river Delaware over against the *Shawna Town*, containing 146 acres. The third tract or Island situated between the creeks or small Branches of the said River Delaware and bounded by the same and the adjacent land to the southward being lately held by John Smith, and that to the Northward is the said Shawna Town, containing 31 acres." These bounds are certainly obscure, and it is hard to tell whether this town or Indian settlement is included; but it is immaterial, though in a time of peace it was certainly very closely encompassed. In it is this strange proviso, that betrays something wrong: "The said three islands or tracts of land hereby granted or mentioned to be granted, with their appurtenances, unto the said Nicholas Depue, his heirs and assigns, against him the said William Allen and his heirs and the heirs of the said William Penn, Esq., and against all and every other person and persons whatsoever Lawfully claiming or to claim by, from or, under him, them, or any of them, shall and will warrant and forever defend by these presents." Here is evidence, that should the Indians resist or attempt at any time to retake said Islands by force, the said Allen and the Penns "would warrant and forever defend" it against all others except those holding from him. Judging by this, the great land speculator must have had something similar from the proprietaries. The aforesaid Indian town was no doubt the same spoken of by Thomas Budd in 1685, which he says was called the Minesinks, immediately on the river side, in a rich section of country and about eighty miles above the falls of the Delaware. Van Der Donck goes still farther back, and mentions it in 1656. From time immemorial, this section was a favorite hunting ground of the Indians, who would not therefore be readily induced to part with it.

These operations were so extensive that we shall now only briefly notice them while going superficially over the records. There was also a considerable tract of land laid out for the same purchaser about the same time by said Surveyor General, about twenty-four miles above the Blue Mountains, from which Mr. Allen, in 1751, sold thirty-one acres to Andrew Dingman, who established here what has been so long known as Dingman's Ferry. The forming of this tract no doubt was why the line from the end of the Walk was made to run at right angles so as to terminate about the mouth of the Lackawaxen, and would then be embraced inside of said limits, and be rid of Indian claims. This we believe has heretofore escaped all writers on the Indian Walk—that Allen held lands so far up nine years before said occurrence. "*By order of John, Thomas and Richard Penn*," there was surveyed and located five thousand acres of land "situated in the Forks of the Delaware River, according to a draft of Benjamin Eastburn, surveyor general." This tract was conveyed by James Logan and Peter Lloyd, attorneys for Letitia Aubrey, to Mr. Allen, on the 10th of April, 1735, and by him sold for twenty-two hundred pounds sterling "to George Whitefield of the Province of Georgia, April 30, 1740." This purchase appears, by tracing the title, to have formed the present township of Upper Nazareth, and in which also the town of Nazareth is situated, being a very desirable tract.

In regard to the latter transaction, John Heckewelder (Hist. Indian Nations, Phila., 1819, p. 337), gives us the following additional information: " In the year 1742, the Rev. Mr. Whitefield offered Nazareth Manor, as it was then called, for sale to the United Brethren. He had already begun to build upon it a spacious stone house, intended for a school house for the education of negro children. The Indians, in the meanwhile, loudly exclaimed against the white people for settling in this part of the country, which had not yet been legally purchased of them, but, as they said, had been obtained by fraud. The brethren declined purchasing any lands on which the Indian title had not been properly extinguished, wishing to live in peace with all the Indians around them. Count Zinzendorff happened at that time to arrive in the country; he found that the agents of the proprietaries would not pay the Indians the price which they asked for that tract of land; he paid them out of his private purse the whole of the demand which they made in the height of their ill temper, and moreover gave them permission to abide on the land, at their village, where they had a fine large peach orchard, as long as they should think proper." He then mentions that, owing to their highly respected chief, Tademi, being murdered by a white man, together with the threats of other persons ill disposed towards them, was the cause of leaving their settlement on this manor, and removing to places of greater safety. These statements are also corroborated by Loskiel in his History of Indian Missions, Crantz's History of the Moravians, and Spangenberg's Life of Count Zinzendorf.

Thomas Penn, by a warrant given at Philadelphia, February 24, 1736, directs the aforesaid Surveyor General to further lay off and survey for Mr. Allen, " 3000 acres in six parcels or tracts of 500 acres each, situate upon or near the West Branch of the Delaware in our county of Bucks, for which he has paid 465 pounds current money and has requested us to issue our Warrant to establish said surveys." These tracts, it is believed, were situated in or near the present towns of Bethlehem and Allentown. We find also at the same time other tracts were surveyed in the same vicinity;

as, for instance, two thousand acres to Thomas Graeme, two thousand acres to James Bingham, fifteen hundred to Caspar Wistar, one thousand to James Hamilton, and one thousand to Patrick Greeme. The conduct of Allen has been pretty severely handled by Charles Thomson in his "Alienation of the Indians," and by Sherman Day, as well as by other writers, and we believe his course has never been defended even by his friends. His life, however, had its vicissitudes, for after being chief justice of the province for twenty-four years, on account of his tory principles, he fled at the commencement of the Revolution to England, where he died an exile to his native land. We find by the records that Thomas Penn granted to Ferdinand John Paris and John Page, his particular friends and attorneys, residing in London, fifteen-hundred acres each. That of the former was located on the Delaware, about six or eight miles above the present town of Easton, and the other we believe between the present towns of Bethlehem and Nazareth. It appears also, that in the following year considerable was surveyed and laid off to purchasers and settlers in the vicinity of the latter place, by Nicholas Scull as deputy for Benjamin Eastburn.

In a joint letter from John, Thomas and Richard Penn, in England, to James Logan, dated January 20, 1731, is found this extract: "We observe what you write about the warrant to John Page and we only give it to secure him that land when the Indian Claims can be taken off. He himself tells us he would much rather lose the land than it should occasion disputes between the Indians and us and we think it very reasonable that after that is made easy he should have it, for which purpose we have given him fresh warrants endorsed on the back that they are not to operate till those disputes are settled and then the surveyor is immediately to finish and return the survey." "The Manor of Chawton," Mr. Page's tract of fifteen-hundred acres, was patented to him, September 11, 1735, and located between the Hockendauqua creek and the Lehigh. The patent for Mr. Parris' tract was given at the same time, and mentions "that in consideration of the many faithful services to us rendered and as an instance of our friendship and regard to him." The requirement, however, was to pay a yearly quit-rent of one shilling sterling, for every one-hundred acres. Recorded in Patent Book A., vol. 7, p. 68, September 18, 1735. What a deliberate falsehood is here exposed by their own statements.

We have been struck by the various ingenious efforts at this time used by the principal actors to conceal the dates of their transactions, so as to cover the nature of the offences. As an instance the following abridgment from the Bucks county records: "On the 5th of December, 1740, for the consideration of £100 currency, William Allen and wife Margaret convey to Issac Iselstein of Bucks county, yeoman, 178 acres, and an island containing about 10 acres, in said West Branch of Delaware River, which said Tract and island were laid out to the said William Allen under the right of John and Ann Sharlot Lowther to 5000 acres in the Province aforesaid, with all houses and improvements." As this was Mr. Allen's deed, we must conclude that it was his work, and will equally apply to him in quite a number of other cases. This grant no doubt was made to him sometime before the Walk of September, 1737. However, this appears more obvious in the records and documents of Thomas Penn, and which have so lately passed out of the family, after being so long and closely kept. They are complete from 1701 to 1779, with the exception of from July 2, 1736, to November, 1738, which are wholly missing, and were no doubt intentionally destroyed between the years 1756 and 1759, to prevent investigation and exposure. Transactions between March 23, 1729, and September 10, 1735, are lumped together, but before and after these dates they are readily understood, and names of purchasers, dates, areas and localities, are fully specified.

A letter was sent by the Delaware Indians to Chief Justice Jeremiah Langhorne, dated Smithfield, March 26, 1741, wherein they complain that there was "about one hundred families of whites settled on their lands which these folks say Thomas Penn had sold them the land. If he has it never was his to sell, that their lands extend down along the Delaware to the mouth of the Tohickon, thence up said stream to its very source, thence by a straight line to Patquating, and thence by a straight line to the Blue Mountains, thence to a place called Mahaning, thence along a mountain called Nessamack, thence along the great swamp to a branch of Delaware river, and so to the Delaware to the place of beginning. They state that they had sold the tract at Durham, Nicholas Dupue's and Weiser's tracts, and now desire that Thomas Penn would take these people off from our land in peace, if not that they would be compelled to do it, but would prefer to live in peace and friendship." This in the end proved no idle threat to the unfortunate settlers thereon, for it was here that the Delawares fought with the most determined fury for the recovery of their favorite hunting grounds, of which the avariciousness and trickery of the Penns and their officials had dispossessed them, and that too by force through a connivance with the more powerful Iroquois.

A Council was held with the Indians in Philadelphia, July 6, 1742, by Governor Thomas, at which were present Sassoonan, Nutimus and other chiefs. On this occasion Canassatego, chief of the Onandagoes, made a speech in behalf of the Delawares: "We know," he said, "our lands are now becoming more valuable. The white people think we do not know their value, but we are sensible that the land is everlasting, and the few goods we receive for it are soon worn out and gone. For the future we will sell no lands but when Brother Onas is in the country; and will know beforehand the quantity of the goods we are to receive. Besides we are not well used with respect to the lands still unsold by us. Your people daily settle on these lands and spoil our hunting. We must insist on your removing them, as you know they have no right to settle to the nothward of Kittochtinny Hills. We desire they may forthwith be made to go off the land, for they do great damage to our cousins the Delawares." Here several grave charges are made ; one that they had not received the amount of goods promised them for their lands. We also perceive that he was ignorant of the claim set up by the proprietaries through the Walk to all that section by the extraordinary manner they had the head line extended.

As to the character of Thomas Penn on these matters, Robert Vaux, in a discourse delivered before the Historical Society (Memoirs, Vol. 11, p. 31) January 1, 1827, gives the following account: "The proprietor had several meetings with the Indians, in order to arrange their land affairs, which, however, did not result to their satisfaction. He also, with a view to raise money, devised a lottery for the disposal of one hundred thousand acres of land. This was an original attempt to introduce legalized gambling into Pennsylvania, and though the mischievous plan was frustrated, the mere proposition, seriously, and with good reason, impaired the confidence which some of the people of the province had been wont to repose in the proprietary. Part of the land selected for prizes in the contemplated raffle, lay within the region claimed by the natives, who, on being apprised of the fact, uttered loud complaints, and for the first time threatened to resist any invasion of their territory. Thomas Penn's visit to the province certainly did not contribute to strengthen the friendship of the Indians, and when he returned to England in 1741, the Assembly in addressing him, said 'whatever differences of opinion may have happened between us, we hope thou wilt believe the freemen of the province retain a proper regard for the proprietary.' Plainly showing that a disagreement had existed, and that their separation was not on the cordial terms of their meeting." We see in this statement a resemblance to the final departure of his father in 1701.

CHAPTER IV.

THE TRIAL WALK.

William Penn died July 30, 1718, at the age of 74 years, leaving six children. The Province of Pennsylvania he bequeathed to the three sons of his second marriage, John, Thomas and Richard, giving to the eldest a double portion. John, who thus became the proprietor of one-half the province, died in 1746, and left his whole estate to his brother Thomas. The latter came over to attend to affairs here in August, 1732, and remained till August, 1741; making a stay of nine years. John, the elder brother, arrived here in September, 1734, and returned near the close of that month in the following year to England to oppose the pretensions of Lord Baltimore respecting the boundaries of Maryland. These were the only visits they made here. In the case of John Penn, as will be observed, the stay was quite brief. Thomas Penn was a shrewd, designing, close-fisted business man. His character has been pretty severely spoken of by Benjamin Franklin, Charles Thomson, John F. Watson, Sherman Day and others. He was here in the interval of 1732 and 1741, a very interesting period, and long enough to get sufficiently acquainted to cause considerable trouble to the colonists and the Indians. On his arrival he was thirty-one years of age and old enough to have shown more discretion.

We have said that there had been a great deal of mystery about the Indian Walk; its date, beginning and ending have alike puzzled the ablest minds without thinking there was a design in it. We now come to a still greater mystery, the Trial Walk; the truth of which the private papers of Thomas Penn have at last revealed. The great wonder is how this could be so long and completely kept a secret by those engaged in it; that in the great investigation from 1756 to 1760, or later, on the misgovernment of the Penns, it should have escaped also the notice of such men as Benjamin Franklin, Charles Thomson, Isaac Norris, Israel Pemberton, Thomas Lightfoot, the Friendly Association, and a host of others, so ardently engaged in ferreting out their abuses.

Soon after his arrival, and even sometime before, as we have shown, the attention of Thomas Penn was called by his particular friends to the Indian complaints and the encroachments of speculators and settlers on their lands, which, if not soon satisfactorily adjusted, might terminate in open hostilities and war. In October, 1734, John and Thomas Penn, by appointment, met the Indians at Durham, where a company had purchased a desirable tract containing six thousand acres, before 1727, and erected iron works thereon. As James Logan, one of the proprietary commissioners of property, and William Allen, of whom we have already spoken, were among these purchasers, it may not appear so strange that on dividing it December 24, 1773 (Bucks Co. Records, Deed Book F, p. 192), it was found *to contain eight thousand five hundred and eleven acres and one hundred perches.* What was said and done at the meeting here has never been made public. It is known that Tishcohan and Nutimus were present, and that the preliminaries relating to the Indian Walk *must have been arranged,* and another meeting agreed upon the following spring at Pennsbury. But before that meeting was to take place a trial or experimental walk was determined on as quietly as possible, and, of course, unknown to the Indians. Without further introduction we are now brought to this subject.

The earliest mention we have found relating in any way to this Walk, is in an account of having paid "April 12, 1735, Timo. Smith, Expenses on travelling ye Indian Purchase £5," and six days afterwards for "sundries" sent the same £2 s11. The gentleman here mentioned was a resident of the present township of Upper Makefield, and at this time the high sheriff of Bucks county, owing his commission to his employer, who had appointed him, with James Steel his receiver general, to conduct and oversee this walk with the assistance of John Chapman, of Wrightstown, deputy surveyor of the county. Smith, with his assistants, must have commenced near the beginning of April to locate and clear the route for travelling the line. To a manuscript book (p. 137), written by John

Watson, afterwards deputy surveyor of the same county, we are indebted for some important information which he copied from Chapman's memoranda made while engaged in this work:

"From Wrightstown, where the first Indian purchase came to, to Plumstead, is a little to the North of the North West along the Road 9 or 10 miles, and the several Cources of the Road from Plumstead to Catatuning Hills (Blue Mountain) is North West 8 miles to the head of Perkiomen Branch, North West by North 4 miles to Stokes' Meadow, North 1 mile by the old Draught, North North West 16 miles to the West Branch, then by the same North 30 chains, North North West 25 chains, North West 6 chains, North 90 chains, North North West 117 chains, North 74 chains, North North East 30 chains, North West by North 410 chains to the Mountain. Begun to be run or surveyed 22d of 2 Mo. and ended the first of May in the year according to English Account, 1735, by John Chapman. Almost a copy by Jno. Watson."

From the aforesaid we obtain the following: That from Wrightstown to Plumstead is 9 or 10 miles, from the latter place to the head branch of Perkiomen 8 miles, to Stokes' Meadow 4 miles, and to the West Branch or Lehigh river 17 miles, making, from Wrightstown to the Lehigh, 39 miles, and to the Lehigh Gap of the Blue Mountain a total of 48¾ miles. These facts prove that this route was laid through Bedminster township near the present village of Strawntown, keeping west of the Haycock, or it would not have passed over the head of Perkiomen and through Stokes' Meadow, which was the place lately owned and occupied by General Paul Applebach. By comparing the line of this route with late maps it will be found on a pretty direct course towards the Lehigh Gap.

It would appear that these preparations involved so much time and labor that John and Thomas Penn became uneasy, and James Steel was instructed to write, April 26th, to Timothy Smith as follows: "The Proprietaries are impatient to know what progress is made in travelling over the land that is to be settled in the ensuing treaty that is to be held with the Indians at Pennsbury on the fifth day of the next month, and therefore desire thee, without delay, to send down an account of what has been done in that affair, and if anything is omitted or neglected which should have been pursued, the same may be yet performed before the intended time of meeting the Indians." Only three days after this he sends another letter to Smith and Chapman, in which he says: "The Proprietaries are very much concerned that so much time hath been lost before you begun the work recommended so earnestly to you at your leaving Philadelphia, and it being so very short before the meeting at Pennsbury, the fifth of the next month, that they now desire that upon the return of Joseph Doane, he together with two other persons who can travel well should be immediately sent on foot on the day and half journey, and two others on horse-back to carry necessary provisions for them and to assist them in their return home. The time is now so far spent that not one moment is to be lost; and as soon as they have travelled the day and half journey, the Proprietaries desire that a messenger may be sent to give them account, without delay, how far that day and half travelling will reach up the country. Pray use your utmost diligence, and let nothing be wanting to be done on this important occasion, which will give great satisfaction to the Proprietaries, who will generously reward you, and those you employ, for your care and trouble."

What do these confidential extracts reveal: "Let nothing be wanting to be done on this important occasion, which will give great satisfaction to the Proprietaries, who will generously reward you and those you employ." No foul means are asked, but anyhow, so it be done to the advantage of the employers. The exact date of this one and a half day's walk it has been impossible for us to fix, but it is believed from some of the attending circumstances, that it was made between the first and eighth of May. Neither can we positively give the names of the three walkers, but no doubt they were Edward Marshall, Joseph Doane and probably James Yates. In a letter from Steel to Smith, dated the 27th of August, 1737, relative to the final walk, we find an intimation that Marshall was certainly meant—"and for that purpose our Proprietor would request thee to speak to that man of the three which travelled and held out the best when they walked over the land before, to attend that service at the time mentioned." We have thought in consequence of Edward Marshall being a chain carrier for either Benjamin Eastburn, surveyor general, or Nicholas Scull, his deputy, or perhaps for both, may have led to his being appointed one of the walkers. The fact would be certainly interesting could it be ascertained what brought his engagement about.

The Penn accounts state that Timothy Smith was paid twice for going over this walk, the second time, May 31st, £10, we suppose for attending the walkers. We next find that he was paid for "ye 3 men who travelled ye Purchase £15," which, in our present currency, is about $11 to each one. John Watson, Sr., of Buckingham, in his communication on the Walk in 1815, is correct in the following extract if applied to this walk, though like all other writers heretofore on the subject, ignorant of this experimental trip: "In the spring of the year 1735, a surveyor employed for the purpose run and measured a line beginning where the northwest boundary of the first purchase crossed the Durham road, and thence northwesterly on the said road to somewhere about Haycock, and then turned more to the left thro' the woods to the Lehigh Gap in the Blue mountain, blazing the southeast side of the trees and saplings in the woods within sight of each other."

We have both the authority of James Steel and Timothy Smith, that Thomas Penn selected the walkers, though, as we shall show hereafter, he professed an entire ignorance on the subject. Steel's letters also prove that before undertaking the charge of the Trial Walk, Timothy Smith and John Chapman had both been to Philadelphia and *received their instructions from one or both of the proprietaries, how to conduct and carry it out to their satisfaction.* In the testimonies of several that were present at the final Walk of 1737, we find some allusions to this, but without the aforesaid information could not have been well understood. Timothy Smith, on his affirmation, says that he was employed "the May preceding [1735] the going the said Walk to get some persons to try the course in order that the said Walk might go by a straight Line as near as it could, he accordingly did with some other Persons try the proposed course by as near a straight Line as they well could, but it leading them over the Mountains and thro' a very rocky broken way which as this affirmant conceived, could not answer, he therefore advised that in going the said Walk they should keep the great Road and old Paths as much as might be." From a personal knowledge, there is no question that this route did lead through an uncommonly rocky country, particularly in the present townships of Haycock and Springfield, and in fact almost to the Lehigh, which was a serious impediment to opening the road as laid out for travel.

Ephraim Goodwin, of Springfield township, who was present at the Walk of 1737, in his testimony, says: "There had been, as he was informed, a course by marked trees, run and laid out previous to going the said walk." John Heider, another witness of 1737, says, after passing through Lehigh Gap they continued the walk a northwest course for seven or eight miles, "by trees which had been marked for a good part of the Way." Alexander Brown, of Buckingham, also affirms that in going from George Wilson's plantation, believed to be near the present village of Springtown, to Lehigh, they sometimes went "by an old path and sometimes by marked trees which he understood had been made sometime before by the surveyors, who, as this affirmant heard and understood, had tryed the course that the said walkers were to go, and where there were neither roads and paths to walk in, had marked trees to direct them in the straight course to avoid hills." Joseph Knowles, a nephew of Timothy Smith, who lived with him at this time, in speaking of the Walk of 1737, says: "I went sometime before to carry the chain, and to help to clear a road as directed by my uncle." Moses Marshall, the son of Edward, related to John Watson, Jr., in 1822, that he had learned from his father that a line "had been run and marked for them to walk by to the top of the Blue Mountain." In all this testimony how ingeniously the Trial Walk has been kept concealed.

The Trial Walk, as stated, came off in the beginning of May, 1735, and what is popularly denominated the Indian Walk not till the 19th and 20th of September, 1737. As will be seen, this experimental walk was made two years and about four months previously. The leading object of this was no doubt to ascertain first how far said walk might extend up into the country, and in consequence be the better prepared to deal with the Indians on this matter at Pennsbury, where a meeting had been appointed to be held the previous summer. James Steel's letters to Timothy Smith clearly reveal how anxious and impatient the proprietaries had become to have the Walk made and reported to them in time for the Pennsbury meeting, which took place the 9th of May, 1735, immediately afterwards, at which Lapowinzo, Nutimus, Tiscohan and other Indians were present; the same who met in Philadelphia in August, 1737, when the deed was made and signed in the presence of Thomas Penn and then determined to be publicly walked out.

The chief object of the Trial Walk was no doubt to make it certain of going far enough up into the country, and by drawing a line at right angles from its extremity, to take in all the desirable lands for a considerable distance above the Blue Mountains along the Delaware, even, if necessary, to the mouth of the Lackawaxen, where, as we have stated, the Penns had sold thousands of acres to William Allen and others as early as 1728, without any regard to honor, justice or the rights of the Indians; yea, *without even their knowledge or consent*.

From the testimony of the witnesses present at the Walk of 1737, we get considerable information respecting this; for instance, that it was laid out by a compass and made as direct as possible, and where there were no roads or paths trees were marked to indicate the proper direction for the walkers. According to the affidavit of John Heider, the trees had been marked for seven or eight miles beyond the Lehigh Gap. So we can be sure of this Walk having at least gone that far, but more likely some distance beyond.

There is no question that this Walk has puzzled writers by being confounded with the one of 1737. For instance, John Watson, Sr., who was once the possessor of the manuscript book of John Watson, the deputy county surveyor, by the information contained therein, was led into the error that the real or final Walk had taken place in the spring of 1735. The secrecy of this affair for so long an interval was really wonderful, and cannot in any way redound to the credit of those engaged in it. If done in the first place through ignorance of its ultimate objects, the Walk of 1737 *must have revealed to them* the nature of the business they had been engaged in and the consequences that must surely follow. John Chapman died in 1743, and Timothy Smith at a very advanced age in the spring of 1776, and we suppose the descendants of their old neighbors in Upper Makefield and Wrightstown townships have no traditions respecting it, as appears to be verified in the writings of John Watson, Sr., Joseph Smith, John Watson, Jr., Samuel Preston, Charles B. Trego, Dr. Charles W. Smith, Thomas Warner, Michael H. Jenks, Benjamin Wiggins, and others of that vicinity. That there was an experimental walk is proved beyond a doubt, and the secrecy that so long enveloped it bodes that it was not done for any good or noble purpose.

CHAPTER V.

THE WALKING PURCHASE.

The Swedes arrived in the Delaware in 1638 with two vessels under the command of Peter Minuet. They brought a number of colonists with provisions, ammunition and merchandise for traffic, and first landed at a spot near Cape Henlopen, which was called Paradise. The colonists conciliated the natives, and purchased from them the land on the west side of the bay from Cape Henlopen to Sankhicon, or the falls at Trenton. This they called New Sweden. Minuet, as well as those who succeeded him, sedulously cultivated peace with the natives. The Dutch, having wrested the country from the Swedes in 1655, were succeeded nine years after by the English, and its government vested in that of New York. A purchase was made from four Indian chiefs in 1679, in the name of Sir Edmund Andros, governor of the colony, for the Duke of York, of a tract in the present Bucks county, extending as far as eight or nine miles above the falls, and about the same distance below, without exactly defining the limits westward.

The next purchase of lands above the Neshaminy was most probably made by William Markham, as the agent of William Penn, on the 15th of July, 1682; nearly four months before the arrival of the latter. It was made with thirteen chiefs, and appears to have been in part based on the purchase of 1679. It was to extend from a white oak on the land in the tenure of John Wood, opposite the falls of Delaware, and to go thence up the river side to a corner spruce tree, marked with the letter P, at the foot of a mountain, and from the ledge or foot of said mountain west-southwest to a corner white oak, marked with the letter P, standing by the Indian path leading to an Indian town called Playwicky, and near the head of a creek called Towsisnick; thence westward to the Neshaminy and along the same to its mouth; then up the river Delaware aforesaid to the white oak on John Wood's land. Though its upper limits are so vaguely defined, we believe the genuineness of this conveyance has never been questioned. It would extend from somewhere in or adjacent to Wrightstown to the foot of the hills on the south side of the Lehigh.

On the 17th of September, 1718, a deed of release was given by sundry Delaware Indian chiefs, Sassoonan and six others, for all the lands situated between the rivers Delaware and Susquehanna, and on the south from Duck creek to the mountains this side of Lehigh, with an acknowledgment that they had *seen and heard divers deeds of sale read unto them*, under the hands and seals of former kings and chiefs of the Delaware Indians, their ancestors and predecessors, who were the owners of these lands, by which they had granted the lands to William Penn, for which they were satisfied and content, which, for a further consideration of goods delivered them, they then confirmed. This was recorded May 13, 1728, yet the Penns made no use of these deeds.

We now come to the preliminaries attending the Walking Purchase; on what it was based, and how it was finally agreed upon by the proprietaries and Indians, with the proceedings connected therewith as set down at the time with the approbation of Thomas Penn. We know that it has been said that Penn was not present, and in the examination in 1756–59 he tried to leave this impression in his writings, with the evident design to clear himself by throwing whatever blame there might be on his agents. Turning to the Pennsylvania Archives (Vol. I, pp. 539 to 543), we shall find what is now wanted. That a council was held with the Delaware Indians at Philadelphia, August 24, 1737, at which was present "The Hon'ble Tho's Penn, Esqr., Prop'r," James Logan, Esq., President, and Samuel Preston, Clement Plumstead, J. Lawrence, Richard Assheton, I. Hasell, J. Griffitts, Alexander Hamilton, and William Allen, of the Council.

"The Proprietor informed the Gentlemen present, that his Elder Brother and himself, having some time since had two Meetings with the Delaware Indians, one at Durham, and the other at Pennsbury, not only for the Renewal of Friendship with the People, but likewise to adjust some Matters relating to Lands lying in the county of Bucks, which tho' formerly fully and absolutely, released by the Indians, then inhabiting those Parts, to his Father, yet they had of late made some claim to them. That the Indians who met at Pennsbury, having represented that some of their Chiefs were then absent, who ought to be consulted on the Occasion, nothing was then concluded on; but that now a great number of those Indians, with several of their Chiefs and ancient Men, were come hither to proceed on the Business, and he the Proprietor had given the Gentlemen the trouble of meeting to hear what is offered; but that the whole might be the better understood, several Papers containing what had passed at Pennsbury were read.

"The Indians being then called in and seated, they were thus spoke to, Barefoot Brunston being Interpreter. That on the Proprietor Thomas Penn's coming into the Country, he was very desirous of seeing his Brethren the Delaware Indians; that on his elder Brother John Penn's coming hither, he had likewise the same Inclination, and they, the Proprietaries, together, had once met those Indians at Durham, and afterwards at Pennsbury; that they could have wished to have seen those old Men who are now here at those Meetings; that nevertheless, they are now pleased to see them, are always glad of such opportunities to renew the old League and Friendship that had been established with them.

"That all the Indians must be fully sensible as well of the Justice of William Penn as of his great love for all the Indians, since he made it a Rule, constantly to be observed, neither to take possession himself, nor suffer others to possess themselves of any Lands without first purchasing them from the Indians, who had a right to them. That when William Penn's sons saw the Indians at Durham, they mentioned the old friendship which their Father had established with all the Indians, and entered into some discourse about the Lands lying—[Here is left a blank space, for what purpose will be shown hereafter]. That at Pennsbury these Matters were again spoken of fully, but as several of the Indians now here were not then present, it might be convenient that they should hear what then passed.

"And the speech of May 8th was read and interpreted to them, Upon producing the Deeds referred to in that speech, to wit: one from Mayhkeerukkisho, &c., dated the 28th of August, 1680, and the other from Idquhon and several southern Indians, dated 15th July, 1682. The Indians now fully acknowledged and owned the last mentioned Deed to be true, and added that they had not a sufficient knowledge of it when they were at Pennsbury; but having since conferred with some of the ancient Men of the Southern Indians, they are convinced of the truth of it. As to the other Deeds, the Indians making some Hesitation, the same was not only read and fully interpreted to them, but likewise the Deposition of Joseph Wood, who was present at the said sale, and has signed as a Witness to the Deed, and likewise the Deposition of William Biles, who was present at this transaction, and remembers well all that then passed; and the whole matter being fully stated to the Indians, they desired till the afternoon to consider the same.

"P. M. The Proprietor, President and several Gentlemen of the Council, being met, the Indians came, and being seated, Manawkyhickon, their speaker, delivered himself thus by the Interpreter. That he is much rejoiced to see the Proprietor, whose Father was a good Man, and in his stead his son now stands; that being desirous to preserve and continue the same Love and Friendship that had subsisted between William Penn and all the Indians, he now presents the Proprietor with a belt of Wampum of four Rows; that he should be sorry if after this mutual Love and Friendship anything should arise that might create the least misunderstanding, which they will carefully endeavor to avoid. That the Proprietor knows well how the Lines mentioned in the deeds from Mayhkeerichshoe, &c., are to run; but they do not fully understand them.

"Hereupon, a Draught was made, and the same being explained to the Indians, and they conferring together, their speaker proceeded and said: That upon considering all that they had heard touching the said Deed, and now seeing the Lines in it laid down, they are sufficiently convinced of the truth thereof, and that they have no objection, but are willing to join in a full and absolute Confirmation of the said sale. That, nevertheless, as the Indians and white People have ever lived together, in a good understanding they, the

Indians, would request that they may be permitted to remain on their present settlements and Plantations, tho' within that purchase, without being molested. In answer to which the assurances that were given on this head at Pennsbury, were repeated and confirmed to them, and the Proprietor told them he would speak further to them to-morrow."

DEED AUTHORIZING THE WALK.

We, Teeshakomen, *alias* Tisheekunk, and Nootamis, alias Nutimus, two of the Sachemas or Chiefs of the Delaware Indians, having almost three years ago, at Durham, begun a Treaty with our honourable Brethren John and Thomas Penn, and from thence another Meeting was appointed to be at Pennsbury, the next Spring following, to which We repaired with Lappawinzoe and several others of the Delaware Indians, At which Treaty several Deeds were produced and Showed us by our said Brethren, concerning Several Tracts of Land which our Forefathers had, more than fifty years ago, Bargained and sold unto our good Friend and Brother William Penn, the Father of the said John and Thomas Penn, and in Particular one Deed from Maykeerickkisho, Sayhoppy and Taughhaughsey, the Chiefs or Kings of the Northern Indians on Delaware, who, for large Quantities of Goods delivered by the Agents of William Penn, to those Indian Chiefs, Did Bargain and Sell unto the said William Penn, All those

Tract or Tracts of Lands lying and being in the Province of Pennsylvania, Beginning upon a line formerly laid out from a Corner Spruce Tree, by the River Delaware, about Makeerickkitton, and from thence running along the ledge or foot of the Mountains, West South West to a corner White Oak marked with the letter P, Standing by the Indian Path that leadeth to an Indian Town called Playwicky, and from thence extending Westward to Neshaminy Creek, from which said line the said Tract or Tracts thereby Granted doth extend itself back into the Woods as far as a man can goe in one day and a half, and bounded on the Westerly side with the Creek called Neshaminy, or the most Westerly branch thereof, so far as the said Branch doth extend, and from thence by line ─────────── to the utmost extent of the said one day and a half's Journey, and from thence to the aforesaid River Delaware, and from thence down the Several Courses of the said river to the first mentioned Spruce Tree. And all this did likewise appear to be true by William Biles and Joseph Wood, who upon their affirmations, did solemnly declare that they well remembered the Treaty held between the Agents of William Penn and those Indians. But some of our Old Men being then Absent, We requested of our Brethren John Penn and Thomas Penn that we might have more time to Consult with our People concerning the same, which request being granted us, We have, after more than two years since the Treaty at Pennsbury, now come to Philadelphia, together with our chief Sachems Monockyhickon, and several of our Old Men, and upon a further Treaty held upon the Subject, We Do Acknowledge Ourselves and every of Us, to be fully satisfied that the above described Tract or Tracts of Land were truly Granted and Sold by the said Mayhkeerickkishsho, Sahoppy, and Taughhaughsey, unto the said William Penn and his Heirs, And for a further Confirmation thereof, We, the said Monockyhickon, Lappawinzoe, Tisheekunk, and Nutimus, Do, for ourselves and all other the Delaware Indians, fully, clearly, and Absolutely Remise, Release, and forever Quit claim unto the said John Penn, Thomas Penn, and Richard Penn, All our Right, Title, Interest, and pretensions whatever of, in, or to the said Tract or Tracts of Land and every Part and Parcel thereof, So that neither We, or any of us, or our Children, shall or may at any time hereafter, have Challenge, Claim, or Demand any Right, Title, Interest, or pretensions whatever of, in, or to the said Tract or Tracts of Land, or any Part thereof, but of and from the same shall be excluded, and forever Debarred. And We do hereby further Agree, that the extent of the said Tract or Tracts of Land shall be forthwith Walked, Travelled, or gone over by proper Persons to be appointed for that Purpose, According to the direction of the aforesaid Deed. In Witness whereof, We have hereunto set our hands and Seals at Philadelphia, the Twentyfifth day of the Month called August, in the Year, Ac-

cording to the English Account, one thousand seven
hundred and thirty-seven.

> MANAWKYHICKON, his x mark,
> LAPPAWINZOE, his x mark,
> TEESHACOMIN, his x mark,
> NOOTAMIS, his x mark.

"It was therefore necessary," remarks Charles Thomson in his Alienation of the Indians (p. 36), "in order that things might be carried on quietly, that the Deed of 1718 should be passed over in silence, and that *Sassoonan* should not be present, nor any of those who signed that Deed. If it be asked what advantage could be gained by getting the Deed of 1686 confirmed, we shall easily see by an account of the Walk, and of the advantage taken of the Blanks in the Deeds of release. Great stress is laid on a Deed (ib., pp. 47, 48), said to be granted above fifty-five years ago. This is said to be the Deed of 1686. Yet, tho' it is mentioned here as lying on the Table; nay, tho' the Indian Speaker says that he had seen it with his own Eyes, yet still it is doubted whether there really was such a Deed. It is certain there is none such now in being, nor recorded: For, at the Treaty at *Easton*, 1757, when the Indian King demanded that the Deeds might be produced, by which the Proprietors held the lands, and the Governor and his Council determined to follow the Course the Proprietor had chalked out, and to justify their claim by the Deed of 1686, and the Release of 1737, they had no deed of 1686 to produce:

but instead thereof, produced a Writing, said to be a copy of that Deed, not attested, nor even signed by any one as a true Copy. From whence some have been ready to conclude that the Charge brought by the *Indian* chief, at the Easton Treaty in 1756, is not without grounds; where he says, that some lands were taken from him by Fraud and Forgery; and afterwards, when called upon to explain what he means by the Terms, says, 'When one Man had formerly Liberty to purchase Lands, and he took a Deed from the *Indians* for it, and then dies; and after his Death the Children forge a deed like the true one, with the same Indian names to it, and thereby take Lands from the *Indians* which they never sold.—This is Fraud.' It is further asked, if there was such a Deed, why was it not recorded as well as the Release of 1737 answering thereto? A Paper (ib., p. 128), said to be a Copy of a Deed, dated 28th of 6th Month 1686, and endorsed, 'Copy of the last Indian Purchase.' To give it some Credit, it has been confidently asserted, that the said Indorsement is of the Hand-Writing of William Penn; but on its being produced at *Easton*, and examined, it appeared clearly, and was confessed by the Secretary and several others acquainted with Mr. Penn's Hand-Writing, not to be his, nor indeed is it like it. Its chief Mark of Credit is that it appears to be ancient Paper. But there is no certificate of its being a Copy, nor was it ever recorded. As the name of *Joseph Wood* is put as one of the Evidences, and as a Person of that name declared at Pennsbury in

1734, he was present at an *Indian* Treaty in 1686, and it is not known there was any other of that Name, it seems extraordinary if this be a genuine Copy, that he was not then called upon to make some Proof of it."

No one, we believe, has ever pretended that the Deed of 1686 was not a forgery. Such it appears from our observations to have been, and different writers have pronounced it so. This deed, whatever worth, was brought to light by Thomas Penn, and in his correspondence he confessed that the original could not be found. It was highly important for him to go by this document on account of its blanks, in the filling of which he might turn the Walk to the highest possible advantage. In a letter from Philadelphia to his brothers John and Richard in England, dated August 20, 1737, but five days before the walking purchase was agreed upon, he says: "I should have acquainted you that just now several of the Delaware Indians who were at Pennsbury when John Penn was here are come, I hope to put an end to the dispute, the particulars of which he is acquainted with." On the 11th of October following he writes again to the same and says: "Since I wrote you last at no very great expence concluded with the Delaware Indians on the Foot of the Agreement made in 1686, *which tho' done to their satisfaction takes in as much ground as any person here ever expected.* I would not take their conveyance as it would have lessened the validity of the former deed, but only a release of their claim with an acknowledgment of their ancestors before mentioned sale." Here is evidence of the importance he attached to that deed, and on which the walk of 1737 is based, and why he had them so firmly bound, even to acknowledgments about which they could have known but little or nothing, admitting it true after upwards of half a century had passed away.

As will be observed, in the Walking Purchase of August 25, 1737, reference is made of the meeting held at Durham in the summer of 1734: "At which Treaty several Deeds were produced and Showed us by our said Brethren, concerning Several Tracts of Land which our Forefathers had more than fifty years ago, Bargained and sold." In this extract some ingenuity is exhibited, for it is impossible to tell what deeds are meant, whether that of 1680, 1682 or 1686, or even others. It is enough to confirm the truth of what Charles Thomson has said in relation to this matter, or else why so skillfully evaded? Again from the same, "not only for the Renewal of Friendship with those People, but likewise to adjust some Matters relating to Lands lying in the county of Bucks, which tho' formerly fully and absolutely released by the Indians, then inhabiting those Parts to his Father, yet they had of late made some claim to them. That all the Indians must be fully sensible as well of the Justice of William Penn as one of his great Love for all the Indians, since he made it a Rule, constantly to be observed, neither to take possession himself, nor suffer others to possess themselves of any lands without first purchasing them from the Indians, who had a right to them." Though this, coming from Thomas Penn, is but self praise, yet it deserves some reply. If all be as here declared, much of what is stated in this work would be untrue though extracted from Penn's own papers.

It is here said that these lands had been "fully and absolutely released" to Thomas Penn's father by the Indians. We challenge the proof! As mentioned, the deed of 1718 is the only exception between 1682 and 1737, yet established from records, and where, in this interval, in the great quantities of lands sold to speculators and settlers, could any regard be exhibited for the rights of the Indians? William Penn, on his second visit here, was so remiss as not to pay any attention to the matter though earnestly pressed by the Assembly. John F. Watson, in his Annals, alluding to John Watson's account of the Walk, says: "He argues, and supposes, that all the country north-west of Wrightstown meeting-house was taken from the Delawares without compensation." This coincides with our views, and nothing, we believe, has ever been established to the contrary.

What did the King, or William Penn, or any of his successors, stipulate to do for the Indians? Go over this chapter and observe closely the transactions connected with the Walking Purchase of 1737, and that instrument itself—how completely one-sided it is! How binding on the Indians, for a consideration *neither specified nor enumerated, yet meant for an equivalent!* Here can be no prejudice exhibited towards the Penns, for it is their own work and will speak for itself. Observe that the Indians "do hereby further agree, that the extent of the said tract or tracts of Lands shall be forthwith walked, travelled, or gone over by proper persons to be appointed for the purpose according to the direction of the aforesaid Deed." From this it would appear that the selection of the walkers was with the consent of both parties, which would have been but justice. Timothy Smith, however, in his affirmation on the Walk of 1737, says: "James Yates, Edward Marshall and Solomon Jennings, who were appointed to go the said walk on the part of the said Proprietaries." Well might it now be asked, where was the authority derived to do this? Not certainly from the release. And, if so desired, why was it not placed there? These are not solitary examples, for the conduct of the several Proprietaries in their intercourse with the Indians exhibits only too many such over-reachings.

Mention is made in the minutes the day before signing the release of the Walking Purchase, "that the proprietor knows well how the lines mentioned in the deed are to run; but they do not fully understand them. Hereupon a draught was made, and the same being explained to the Indians and now seeing the lines laid down, they are sufficiently convinced of the truth thereof, and that they have no objection, but are willing to join in a full and absolute confirmation of the sale." We find further mention of this draft in a letter from Thomas Penn, dated London, April 14,

1759, to William Logan, a member of the Council, in which he says: "We must insist on the terms of the deed and to the day and half's Walk, and as to the course that was laid down in Andrew Hamilton's Draft of the land, by which the deed was explained and which is at right angles with the lower part of the Delaware."

It was our good fortune to find this very draft among the papers of Thomas Penn, by which he attempted to explain to the Indians the proposed course of the Walk. Any one can readily see, on inspecting and comparing it with our present maps, that it was purposely gotten up to deceive. It is a rude affair, on which the Delaware is represented from the mouth of the Neshaminy to the Lehigh river. The forks of the Neshaminy are placed considerably more than half-way towards the Lehigh, when in reality they do not nearly approach half this distance. The "Spruce tree P" is marked on the Delaware a short distance above the "Great Creek Mackerickhitton," from the head of which a line is made westward to the Neshaminy, and serves as a base from the middle of which another line is represented nearly due north with the Lehigh *and no further*, and inscribed "The supposed Day and Half's journey into ye Woods." The deception lies in making this line exactly *parallel with the Delaware*, and not representing it any further to the north or north-northwest. Thomas Penn very well knew, by the Trial Walk, made more than two years previously, that the Lehigh was only half the distance walked, and that the Delaware above it extended towards the northeast, and the further the Walk would reach towards the north-northwest the greater must be the divergence and consequently the amount of territory embraced within it.

The reservation by the Indians, we believe, has hitherto escaped all writers on this subject. We mean the "request that they may be permitted to remain on their present settlements and Plantations, tho' within that purchase, without being molested. In answer to which the assurances that were given on this head at Pennsbury, were repeated and confirmed to them." What an answer to a reasonable request! But it was characteristic of Thomas Penn. Little did they then think that before many years he would employ the Iroquois or Six Nations in New York, regarded by our early writers as the most ferocious Indians inhabiting the New World, to come down on this very tract, and, contrary to ordinance, forcibly eject the Delawares, whose only alternative was to retire to Wyoming with another outrage rankling in their hearts.

In the release of 1737 not an Indian name is given that was on the deed of 1718. We know that Sassoonan, Shickalimy and Civility, distinguished chiefs, were all living at this time. The two former lived for years afterwards, yet it is believed they were in no way consulted, or that they even knew anything about it. William Allen confessed, in an affidavit, that he knew Tedyuscung ten years previously. From other accounts we know he was at this time about thirty-two years of age. Why was he not also consulted? If these were deemed worthy of some consideration on other matters before and after 1737, why not then? The transactions of white men with the Indians have reached us wholly through the hands of the former; therefore, under the most favorable circumstances, it will be still impossible to do them justice. Those who dealt with them, like the Penns, for instance, unfortunately possessed such extraordinary powers as to keep down all expressions of opinion that did not favor them, and which the strong arm of the Revolution could alone overthrow.

CHAPTER VI.

PREPARATIONS FOR THE WALK.

We have in the progress of this work got through with the final adjustment of the Walking Purchase, and now come to the preparations attending it and deemed requisite for a satisfactory consummation.

From the date of the release to the actual Walk was twenty-four days, but had it taken place on the 12th of September, as had been arranged, it would have taken seven days less. From the shortness of the time it will appear that despatch was necessary, so as to bring it to the most successful issue for the proprietaries. John Watson, Jr., about the year 1821, visited Moses Marshall, the son of Edward, then in his eightieth year, and for that age possessed of remarkable memory and understanding, and received from him additional information respecting the Walk, which, as related, he set down. He said that "notice was given in public papers that the remaining day and a half's walk was to be made, and offering five hundred acres of land anywhere in the purchase and £5 in money to the person who should attend and walk the farthest in the given time. By previous agreement the governor was to select three persons and the Indians a like number of their own nation. The persons employed by the governor were Edward Marshall, James Yates and Solomon Jennings. One of the Indians was called Combush, but he has forgotten the names of the other two." We would say that by Governor here is meant Thomas Penn, as his brother John returned to England in 1735, where he remained till his death in 1746. There was at this time no other acting as Governor, though James Logan, president of the Council at this time, was next in rank.

Being desirous of seeing the advertisement relating to the Walk, if in the newspapers of the time, and what reward was really promised, we went over every number of *The Pennsylvania Gazette*, from December 26, 1732–33 to 1738, and *The American Weekly Mercury*, from December 21, 1732–33 to December 28, 1739, without finding it, after devoting several days' labor to this object. In the *Mercury* was an advertisement by Timothy Smith, sheriff, offering a reward for two persons who had broken jail in Bucks county in 1735. This would indicate that if he had done the advertising in the way of offering a reward for the best of three walkers it would have appeared most likely in that paper. These two weekly papers were then the only ones published in Pennsylvania. We do not doubt, however, public notice was given, but it may have been done by written or printed notices posted up at the most public places, along or near the beginning of the Walk; as, for instance, Newtown, then the county seat of Bucks—as it was to the interest of the proprietaries to get the very best and fastest walkers that could possibly be obtained. What Moses Marshall has said on this subject will be regarded as of some authority.

John Heider, a resident of the same county, in his examination on the Walk, says that in the month it came off he was induced to offer himself to be one of the walkers, but was refused by the proprietary officers, when, out of curiosity, he attended to witness its performance. Joseph Furniss, a resident of Newtown, and a near neighbor of James Yates, relates that his situation gave him an easy opportunity to ascertain the time of setting out on the walk; some asserting it was to be made by the river, others that it was to be gone by a straight line somewhere in Wrightstown, opposite a spruce tree on the river's bank said to be the boundary of a former purchase. We see by these statements that as soon as it was generally known the walk was to come off it created some excitement as to its results, but that it must have been pretty quietly conducted we can judge by persons being so puzzled to know when, where and how it was to be performed. Yet Timothy Smith and John Chapman had upwards of two years before opened the way by compass, and had it travelled over and the result reported to the proprietaries, it is supposed, with a view of making sure of securing the Minisink lands to the satisfaction of William Allen and other land speculators, which they had bought some years before, and might not otherwise have been so soon rid of Indian claims.

James Steel, the receiver-general of the proprietaries, and acting under their authority, on the 27th of August, 1737, two days after signing the release of the Walking Purchase, wrote to Timothy Smith as follows: "The treaty which was begun at Durham, and afterwards held at Pennsbury now finished at Philadelphia, and the time appointed for walking over the land is to be the 12th of September next, and for that purpose our Proprietor would request thee to speak to that man of the three which travelled and held out the best when they walked over the land before, to attend to that service at the time mentioned, when Solomon Jennings is expected to join and travel the day and a half with him. Thou art also requested to accompany them, and to provide such provisions for those men as may be needful on the occasion desired. John Chapman is also to go along, and with you—and be sure to choose the best ground and shortest way that can be found. The Indians intend that two or three of their young men shall be present, and see the land fairly walked over." In consequence of the Court of Quarter Sessions being held at Newtown, requiring the attendance of the sheriff as well as some others concerned, the Walk was postponed to the 19th. Notice of this change was at once forwarded to Solomon Jennings to be on hand at the proper time and place and be prepared accordingly.

We see in these letters that Thomas Penn particularly requests Mr. Smith "to speak to that man of the three which travelled and held out the best when they walked over the land before, to attend to that service at the time mentioned." This also shows the great personal interest, if not anxiety, of the proprietary to secure every possible advantage of the Indians. That this walker was Edward Marshall there is no doubt. As additional evidence, he said in his examination in 1757, that Timothy Smith had employed him for the Walk, but by direction of said order. Here is further proof of the characteristic meanness of Thomas Penn, in not afterwards fully compensating him for his hard-earned reward, and thus by serving him too well was to cost him the lives of a wife and son from the long injured and enraged Indians. Samuel Preston, in a visit to Edward Marshall on his island home in 1783, states that he then told him that as a hunter and chain carrier he had been greatly accustomed from his youth to travel on foot, and after he had been appointed to the walk, "he put himself in keeping according to his best judgment fully determined to win the prize of five hundred acres of land where Allentown now stands and the mouth of the Little Lehigh or lose his life in the attempt."

How it came that Edward Marshall, Solomon Jennings and James Yates were appointed it is now difficult to state, but it is well known that they were all three stout, athletic men and distinguished hunters. Marshall was now about twenty-four years of age. Solomon Jennings, we know, had his home at this period in a bend of the Lehigh about two miles above the present town of Bethlehem, being one of the very few whites then living there. The Moravians did not settle in the vicinity till 1741. James Yates, if not a native, must have resided for some considerable time previous in

Newtown township. As Joseph Doane must have undoubtedly participated in the Trial Walk, and why now overlooked, is hard to tell. Jennings, in our opinion, must have been appointed in his place. The four chiefs who signed the release for the Walking Purchase, appointed on their part three Indians whose names were John Combush, Neepaheilomon alias Joe Tuneam, and Tom, his brother-in-law, to accompany the walkers and see that justice was done; as, for instance, that the Walk was fairly performed within the prescribed time, and to note particularly its beginning and termination. Whether Captain Harrison, "a noted Indian," was also selected by them, we are unable to state; but it is certain that he, with Lappawinzo, appeared on their side to take the greatest interest in the matter.

Timothy Smith was particularly charged to accompany the walkers, "and to provide such provisions as may be needful on the occasion. John Chapman is also to go along and be with you,—*and be sure to choose the best ground and shortest way that can be found.* The Indians intend that two or three of their young men shall be present, and see the land fairly walked over." As instructions coming from Thomas Penn, they contain some interesting information, and the most positive proof of a desire to make the very best of it, and, as is always the case, without any injunctions whatever as regards justice or honorable proceedings.

In order to carry out their instructions, Timothy Smith and John Chapman again went over the ground in the beginning of September and gave it a more careful inspection, so as to have the nearest and best possible route for the walkers to travel over, and in so doing made some deviations from that used in the Trial Walk. The route for travel now agreed upon was to start from the place of beginning, near Wrightstown meeting house up the Durham road, to the present village of Stony Point, in Springfield township; thence by the present villages of Bursonville and Springtown, striking the Lehigh river a short distance below Bethlehem. This undoubtedly was a much better selection, thus entirely avoiding the rocky sections of Haycock, Springfield and Saucon. The route of the Trial Walk must have left the Durham road at or near the present village of Gardenville, in Plumstead township, and did not meet again till a short distance this side the Lehigh. With this exception, we believe they were all the same. For this distance they were parallel to each other for about twenty miles, and nowhere beyond four and a half miles apart, which was most likely at the Haycock. Timothy Smith, in alluding to this section and the cause for making the change from a straight line, says: "it leading over the mountains and through a very rocky broken way, conceived that it could not answer, and therefore advised in going the said walk to keep the great road and old paths as much as might be."

It may not prove amiss to make a few additional remarks on the actual condition and improvement of the lower portion of the country through which the Walk was made. The Durham Iron Company was formed March 4, 1727, and composed of some of the wealthiest and most influential men in the province, where they took up in one tract six thousand acres of land on the river Delaware. The iron works were commenced the same year, as well as other extensive improvements. In 1732 they petitioned to the Court of Quarter Sessions for Bucks county, stating that they stood greatly in need of a road leading from there to Bristol, and prayed that one might be speedily granted and opened. It was accordingly laid out that fall from its upper terminus, called Bristol road, below Pidcock's creek, in Buckingham, and extended to the Tohickon, "near where the Deep Run empties into it;" being somewhat over eleven miles in length. This was the origin of the road and why so called. It was not, however, extended as a highway to the Durham Forge till 1746, and nine years afterwards was continued to Easton. So by the information derived from the records, we know that on the line of the Walk in 1737 the public highways did not extend further north than the Tohickon creek, though there was at that time a wagon road from there to the iron works, but which must have been very little travelled, from the sparseness of the population. Yet Marshall, in his examination, calls it "the great Durham road," and which he says was followed "to Gallows Hill," where is now the present village of Stony Point, when they took "a lesser road," and so by paths and marked trees for the remainder of the journey, which extended some seven or eight miles beyond the present Mauch Chunk, or about half-way between that place and where is now the village of White Haven, in Carbon county, terminating only about twenty miles this side the Susquehanna.

CHAPTER VII.

THE INDIAN WALK.

We now come to treat of this celebrated walk, and to make it the more reliable our account of it shall be prepared only from the information transmitted to us by those who were actually present either as participants or witnesses. As aids for this purpose, we possess the narratives of Edward Marshall, Timothy Smith, Alexander Brown, Nicholas Scull, Benjamin Eastburn, John Heider, Ephraim Goodwin, Joseph Knowles, Thomas Furniss and James Steel, who were all present and more or less interested in it. These accounts were nearly all taken down in 1757, twenty years after the occurrence, for the investigation before the King and government of Great Britain into the cause of the Indian wars, and the alleged abuses and misconduct of the Penns in the colony. The long interval that elapsed after the Walk till the general attention became so directed as to collect all facts possible in regard to it on both sides, will account for some of the numerous contradictions which necessarily must occur in such cases, where the testimony is taken apart and by different persons. Our aim has been to collect and diligently compare these various statements, and from the mass to give what appears to be the most reliable with the fullest possible amount of information.

Early on Monday morning, September 19, 1737, an interesting group may have been seen in the Durham road near a large chestnut tree standing on the line and corner of John Chapman's land, but a few rods from Wrightstown meeting house, in Bucks county, brought thither by the sons of William Penn, late Proprietary and Governor of Pennsylvania, with the intention of having walked out a purchase made with the Indians the 25th of August preceding. Timothy Smith, sheriff of the county, had charge of the affair, assisted by Benjamin Eastburn, surveyor general, and his two deputies, Nicholas Scull and John Chapman, also James Steel, Jr., nephew and clerk of the receiver general, who was present from Philadelphia to report to Thomas Penn his observations concerning the matter. Edward Marshall, James Yates and Solomon Jennings were the appointed walkers. To see that the whole would be fairly conducted according to agreement, the Indians had deputed three of their young men to be present, whose names were John Combush, Neepaheilomon, more commonly called Joe Tuneam, who could speak English well, and Tom, his brother-in-law. There were also present Enoch Pearson, one of the brothers of Edward Marshall, Samuel Hughes, and a number of others whose names have not reached us. Precisely at six o'clock, as the sun rose in the eastern horizon, Timothy Smith, by his watch and that of Nicholas Scull, gave the signal to the walkers, who started from the chestnut tree, which had been fixed upon by the proprietaries as the place of beginning, on the day and a half's journey before them, followed by a somewhat motley crowd chiefly on horseback. Timothy Smith had already sent on in advance his nephew, Joseph Knowles, and others, with horses carrying provisions, liquors and bedding for the convenience and comfort of the walkers and his several assistants. They proceeded on the Durham road, and before they got to Buckingham, Joseph Furniss came up with the company, and Alexander Brown joined them in Plumstead.

It appears that near the beginning Yates got somewhat in advance of Marshall, who, in order to overtake him, hurried his steps sufficiently to attract the attention of Joe Tuneam, who cried out in the hearing of John Heider, "that it was not fair." Nothing of particular interest occurred till they arrived about two miles beyond Tohickon creek, at or near Red Hill, between ten and eleven o'clock in the forenoon, when Jennings gave up and joined the rest of the company, with whom he continued till they arrived at the Lehigh, when he left for his home two or three miles distant. When the walkers arrived near Gallows Hill, they turned to the left from the Durham road on an old Indian path through the woods, partly directed by blazed or marked trees, till twelve o'clock, or noon, when they arrived in the meadows of George Wilson, an Indian trader near Durham, or Cook's creek, but now occupied by his widow, where they stopped only fifteen minutes to dine. They then set off again, continuing about the same general course of north-northwest on an old beaten Indian path. Thomas Furniss asserts that during the journey one of the Indians repeatedly expressed his dissatisfaction with the Walk, that it should have gone along the river, and complained of the unfitness of his shoes for travelling, stating that he had expected that Thomas Penn would have made him a present of a pair. As no accommodations whatever, it appears, had been provided for the Indians, some of the company out of compassion let them ride their horses by turns.

The walkers kept on the Indian path and marked trees, crossing Saucon creek and the Lehigh river, then better known as the West Branch of the Delaware, at a ford near the residence of Ebenezer Pettit, a short distance below where is now Bethlehem. This was a little after one o'clock. They followed on the same path leading to the north-northwest. A little after four o'clock, on the authority of Ephraim Goodwin, Marshall, dropping a little behind Yates, hastened his steps for a few paces to come up with him, which Combush observing called to him that he must walk fair. They pursued their journey by paths and marked trees till fifteen minutes past six o'clock in the evening, and extending almost into twilight, the quarter of an hour additional being for the time taken at noon. The two walkers had now been kept twelve hours on their feet, and on the authority of Thomas Furniss, Timothy

Smith, with his watch in his hand, bid them hurry up for a few minutes, as the time was almost out and a piece of rising ground was to be ascended, which they did so briskly that when he announced its expiration Marshall clasped a sapling to support himself. The sheriff asked him what was the matter, when he said he was nearly gone and could not have proceeded much farther.

Where they left off for the day a white oak was marked about half a mile from an Indian town called Hockyondocquay, where Tishecunk, or Tiscohan, lived. They lodged here in the woods this night by ample fires, and heard the shoutings of the Indians at a cantico in the place, to which Combush directed his steps, excusing the party from accompanying him. Tuneam and Tom had left the company several hours before sunset, but were all dissatisfied, saying they were badly cheated, and that the walkers had run and would pass the good land, and did not care how far or where they went to. Next morning brought dull and rainy weather, and to add to their discomforts, several of the horses having strayed away, about two hours were spent in hunting them. On the authority of Edward Marshall, the Indians not appearing, Benjamin Eastburn, Nicholas Scull, and another person, went early in the morning to the Indian town where Lappawinzo lived, and desired him to send some other Indians to accompany them, when he replied that they had got "all the best of the land and they might go to the devil for the bad and that he would send no Indians with them." However, Combush returned with two other Indians, and accompanied them, according to Timothy Smith, for about ten miles, when, the rain increasing, he said he would proceed no farther.

At eight o'clock they started from the place where they had left off in the evening, and continued on the same Indian path till they came to an Indian settlement beyond the Blue Mountains called Pokopogh-cunk, and near the Lehigh river, where a noted Indian called Captain Harrison lived; that from thence they proceeded through the woods in a northwest direction chiefly by marked trees and compasses carried by Marshall, Nicholas Scull and perhaps Benjamin Eastburn, and crossed a large creek which appears to have been the Lehigh, near which Yates gave out from growing "lame and tired," as Timothy Smith says, and which was, according to John Heider, about half an hour before the termination of the Walk. Marshall walked on, accompanied by Alexander Brown, Enoch Pearson, and others, on horseback, till two o'clock in the afternoon, when the time of eighteen hours expired and the north side of the Pocono Mountain was reached, which by some is called the Second or Broad Mountain. Here five chestnut oaks were marked as the extent of the Walk, and on which, according to Benjamin Eastburn, was "cut the Proprietary's name and the year 1737," and also says was "about sixty miles" from the starting place in Wrightstown, but in reality it was considerably more, as will be shown in the following chapter.

Having reached the farthest limits of the Walk, it now remained, through the Proprietary's orders, to run not a direct line, but one at right angles from said five chestnut oaks to the Delaware river, making a distance of about sixty-six miles or more in a northeast direction, and terminating near the mouth of the Lackawaxen. This survey was immediately made under the charge of Benjamin Eastburn, assisted by Nicholas Scull, John Chapman and James Steel, Jr. The receiver general, James Steel, in a letter to the Proprietary, dated Philadelphia, November 28, 1737, thus expresses himself on the subject: "The surveyor-general with my nephew afterwards continued their journey from the upper point or end of the day and half's walk to the river Delaware and which employed them four days." Benjamin Eastburn calls it on his map, "A right line from the end of the day and a half's walk through a mountainous barren country, abounding with pine trees to a Poplar tree by Delaware River marked with the letter P." So in accomplishing about the same distance it cost, by said confession, almost three times the amount of time.

"On the return," relates Thomas Furniss, "we came through this Indian town (Hockyondocquay) or plantation, Timothy Smith and myself riding forty yards. more or less, before the company; and as we approached with about one hundred and fifty paces of the town, the woods being open, we saw an Indian take a gun in his hand, and advancing towards us some distance. placed himself behind a log that laid by our way. I think Smith was surprised, as I well remember I was through a consciousness that the Indians were dissatisfied with the walk, a thing the whole company seemed to be sensible of; and upon the way in our return home frequently expressed themselves to that purpose." In further confirmation of the dissatisfaction expressed by the Indians, Edward Marshall states in his testimony, "that about eight weeks after the performing the walk, happened to be in company with the Indian chief Lappawinzo at the Indian town Hocyondocquay, with Tishecunk and some other Indians, being the first time he had seen them after the said walk. He then heard Lappawinzo say that they were dissatisfied with the walk; and that they would go down to Philadelphia next May with every one a buckskin, to repay the Proprietor what they had received from him and take their land again, and the said Indian complained that the walk was not fairly performed nor the courses run as should have been; and that he has heard Lappawinzo and other Delaware Indians frequently say that the said walk should not go the course agreed on between the Indians and the Proprietors, for they should have went along by the courses of the Delaware or the next Indian path."

CHAPTER VIII.

OBSERVATIONS ON THE WALK.

During the Indian Walk it should be remembered that of the three proprietaries Thomas Penn was alone in this country, his brother John having returned to England about two years previously. So the former must be chiefly responsible for whatever trickery or fraud practiced in carrying it out for his benefit. He was now about thirty-six years of age, certainly old enough to have reformed somewhat over the follies of youth. As regards the Walk from its first conception to the end, it would appear as if he viewed it as a matter out of which a good thing might be made. He, as one of the proprietaries, alone had the right to treat with the Indians, and there was no power in his colony that could call him to account for any abuse. Further, the royal charter, through which he derived this sway, *did not recognize that the Indians had any rights whatever in the soil*, neither did either party in any way ever attempt to civilize, instruct or convert them to christianity, though this had been done to some extent before by the Swedes, and later by the Moravians. But after the breaking out of a long and bloody Indian war, the people, in 1757, as their only recourse, appealed to the king and government of Great Britain for an investigation into the conduct of the proprietaries with the Indians based on Tedyuscung's charge, and were at least partially heard. Now came the cause for hiding away, mystifying, abstracting and prohibiting what should have been public documents. Regarding those matters now from a present standpoint, the question arises, what good had they done to have even merited so long a toleration? One thing is certain, that little justice could be expected from such sources for the colonist and much less for the red man. It was therefore noble in Edward Marshall, though savage vengeance had fallen heavily on his family, to maintain to his latest breath that the Indians had been grossly wronged by the government of the Penns.

For more than a century it has been a matter of dispute where this celebrated Walk did actually begin. We have the authority of Benjamin Eastburn, who was present and acted under the orders of the proprietaries, that it should have commenced at the intersection of the Durham or Bristol road and the township line between Newtown and Wrightstown. This is corroborated by comparing Eastburn's with Thomas Holmes' map of original surveys, commenced in 1682 and filled up for about ten years later. Thomas Furniss, a resident of Newtown township, says: "When the walkers started I was a little behind, but was informed that they proceeded from a chestnut tree near the turning out of the road from Durham road to John Chapman's." Edward Marshall states that they started "from a chestnut tree in the line of John Chapman in Wrightstown." Timothy Smith asserts that the walkers started "from a chestnut tree near the Wrightstown meeting-house." John Heider testifies that the walk was begun "at a tree *within a few rods of* Wrightstown meeting-house, and about four miles from the river Delaware." Ephraim Goodwin says it commenced at Wrightstown meeting-house. Benjamin Eastburn places it at the south corner of John Chapman's (the first settler) tract on the Newtown township line, about three-quarters of a mile from the east corner of Wrightstown township and about *the same distance below the meeting-house.* Should Eastburn be correct, the Towsisnick would prove to be the present Newtown creek. All the aforesaid authorities were present at the Walk.

Joseph Smith, born in 1753, in his account of the Walk, written in 1826, says that when John Chapman ran the line "he marked a chestnut tree three-quarters of a mile below the meeting-house," as the place of beginning, which was no doubt the true starting point. Moses Marshall told John Watson, Jr., in 1822, that his father had told him that the Walk commenced "at the old chestnut tree below Wrightstown meeting-house," but this is not confirmed by his evidence. It is now certain, after weighing all testimony carefully, that the walkers, by direction of those concerned, actually started a few rods above said meeting-house, as has been corroborated by several members of the Chapman family, and which has been concurred in by Dr. Charles W. Smith in his History of Wrightstown, Benjamin Wiggins, Thomas Warner, and also by the late Hon. Michael H. Jenks, of Newtown, who, in a letter to the writer, dated May, 1858, thus expresses himself: "Upon the farm now owned by Edward Chapman once stood the celebrated chesnut tree from which the famous Indian Walk commenced. A chesnut tree is yet pointed out to the curious standing by the side of the old Durham road, as the one alluded to, but this is not the fact. I have seen the stump of the tree some forty years ago, when there were many living to establish the fact." In regard to the upper line, Dr. Smith says that it "is south $43\frac{1}{4}$ degrees west, and is parallel with the southern line of the township, and about a mile north of it." This fact is interesting and shows that there is a mile difference in the two, and it seems to strengthen the evidence with what has been given, that the township line was the proper boundary. Hence our belief, from the authorities given, where the Walk should have honestly commenced, and the further up the actual starting point so much the more of course were the Indians wronged and the walkers enabled the further to extend their journey, adding still more to the catalogue of outrages hitherto named. The conduct of Timothy Smith and John Chapman, life-long residents of that vicinity, in the matter, well deserves consideration.

The route of the Walk as mentioned was on the Durham road, by the present villages of Centreville, Pipersville, Bucksville, Springtown, and crossing the

Lehigh river a short distance below Bethlehem, then through the Lehigh Water Gap, and crossing the said river near the present town of Mauch Chunk, where Yates gave out and Marshall proceeded beyond it, according to Eastburn's map, about four and a half miles, where the Walk terminated on Broad or Second Mountain. The general course was but very little north of northwest. The distance walked in this one and a half day's journey has been variously estimated by different writers. But we need not wonder at this, for the map of the Walk was kept concealed, and whatever else related to the same that might be turned in any way against the interest of Thomas Penn, for which purpose he had in advance carefully instructed those who were his subordinates. Never had a prince more faithful followers, and the result proves that in their selection he was a pretty good judge of character, though, as we shall see, he failed in this matter with William Logan and Benjamin Shoemaker of the Council, and finally with Governor Denny and others, after he had got through with their services. How men otherwise regarded with respect, should have died with such secrets is an absolute wonder, and can only be attributed to their own implication.

John Watson, the surveyor, it appears, some how got access to John Chapman's memoranda, made in the spring of 1735, for the Trial Walk, from which we learn that he surveyed the distance from the starting place to the Blue Mountains, making it forty-eight and three-quarter miles. Edward Marshall, in his examination, estimated the distance walked from the said mountain to the end of the journey, as twenty miles, and John Heider on his oath testifies that Benjamin Eastburn had told him that he had measured the distance and found it seventeen and three-quarter miles, which with John Chapman's survey would make sixty-six and one-half miles, and Marshall's sixty-eight and three-quarter miles. Yet Eastburn, on his map, says that the distance walked by Marshall and Yates "was about sixty miles," as if he had never measured it! This is a very ingenious statement, and will bear several constructions. It may be that the two walkers did together make sixty miles, but to say that they had walked the whole distance would be a direct falsehood, for Yates gave out several miles before Marshall reached the point marked as the termination. Hence another reason for concealing the actual distance. Nicholas Scull, another assistant surveyor present, on his affirmation, said, "that he believes the whole distance walked not to be more than fifty-five statute miles." About the conduct of these surveyors we will have more to say hereafter. They were thus absolutely required to hide or falsify their proceedings to suit their employer, or lose their situations. This is all the information respecting the distance we have been enabled to secure from those who were actually present at the Walk.

Joseph Smith, in his account, makes the distance seventy-two miles; John Watson, Sr., states it to be one day's walk of sixty miles, and John Watson, Jr., on the authority of Moses Marshall, makes it eighty-six miles. On applying the scale on Eastburn's map to the line of the Walk, we made it on the original sixty-five miles, and a friend of ours makes the same sixty and three-quarter miles, the mode of following the curves probably making the difference. Samuel Preston caps the climax by stating that the walk was from sunrise to sunset and the distance estimated from one hundred and ten to one hundred and twenty miles. Our opinion is that the whole distance must have been between sixty-five and seventy-two miles, and we think the aforesaid sixty-six and one-half miles to be the best supported by evidence, and therefore likely to be the most correct. Taking this distance as the true measurement, and made in eighteen hours, it would give very nearly an average of three and three-quarter miles per hour, which is certainly rapid walking. To maintain this speed for a day and a half, or eighteen hours, would be found to be such as few constitutions could endure. We must remember too that after Marshall got twelve miles on his journey, he had, for the want of bridges, to wade all the streams, and that there were no public roads for half the distance, the remainder being on Indian paths and by marked trees through the woods. Several writers, we are aware, have recently said that this walk was no extraordinary performance, and that persons could be found in these degenerate days who could equal if not surpass it. We think it so extraordinary that we should decline attempting it, and which opinion we shall hold till some one of these gentlemen shall show us that they can do as well or better under the circumstances.

From the accounts of Thomas Penn we get some additional information respecting the Walk, as for instance that Timothy Smith was paid September 1, 1737, for a canoe, sixteen shillings; October 5th, for "ye men who travelled ye Purchase £10.3.9"; February 15, 1738, balance of his expenses on the travelling purchase £14.2.5; October 1, 1737, "expenses of B. Eastburn, N. Scull, and J. Steel, Jr., for running ye purchase £17.4.11"; April 1, 1740, "John Chapman, 8 days attending ye Indian purchase £2.8.0." The sum paid Eastburn, Scull and Steel was chiefly for running the head line from the end of the Walk to near the mouth of the Lackawaxen on the Delaware, which cost them four days' labor. John Chapman also assisted, and, as may be seen, was engaged during the whole of this Walk eight days.

After the performance of the Walk, Thomas Penn sent a letter from Philadelphia, dated October 11, 1737, to his brothers in England, of which the following is an extract: "Since I wrote you last, I have at no very great expense concluded with the Delaware Indians on the Foot of the Agreement made in 1686, and with their consent the lands in the upper part of Bucks County have been measured by walking a day and a half's journey, which tho' done to their satisfaction takes in as much ground as any person here ever expected. I would not take their conveyance as it would have lessened the validity of the former deed, but only a release of their former Claim with an acknowledgment of their ancestors before mentioned sale. The Minutes of the Treaty are not settled in so exact a manner as I shall have them reduced to, but I will send you a copy of them with one of the deed by the next ship to London." Having copied this from the original, we would say that he certainly must have attached great importance to this information, from the fact that it occupies the first paragraph enclosed in a brace, and marked "Delaware Indians." He here makes the confession that he had "at no very great expense" accomplished his purposes, and that it takes "in as much ground as any person here ever expected," and that the whole was done "to the satisfaction of the Indians." Who will vouch as to the truth of the last assertion? He here fully exposes himself as to his intentions in having them so strictly bound in the release.

Some time after Thomas Penn's return to England, he wrote from London under date of February 8, 1759, in which he says, "No regular return was made by Benjamin Eastburn, who as the surveyor general was the proper person to make it, but the persons who walked the walk might have signed it." To William Logan, a member of the Council, June 21, 1757, he remarks, "I suppose proper persons used to walk were got, but I hope nothing unfair was done, if there was it was contrary to my knowledge or desire. Those Indians had been very troublesome, and even pretended right to land about Jeremiah Langhornes. I mean Nutimus and his associates, being quite ignorant of former sales. I shall say no more on this subject, but I can assure you, I desire to support my character whenever it is necessary, at the expense of my interest." He here admits that the Indians had been troublesome respecting their lands. As to his hoping that nothing unfair was done in the Walk, it will do very well to say twenty years after the occurrence, when it was about to be investigated by authority of the royal government. In a letter of March 11, 1757, to Richard Peters, he says: "The Deed of 1737 from the Delaware Indians, does not mention any boundary on the north but the line from the end of a Day and an Half's journey to the River Delaware. If their is a release of all their claim in the year 1683, it may be mentioned. But I think we should rely on the bounds of the Day and an Half's walk, which may be estimated to the Kittannin Hills fairly by the walk, and could not be said to run back from the river further than till it met the springs of the Schuylkill Creeks." Here is an admission, twenty years after the Walk, that he was satisfied to have it extend only to the Blue Mountains. Why did he not state this long before? And above all why not confess to the thousands of acres he had sold north of those mountains, between 1727 and the Walk as mentioned in a previous chapter? To William Logan, he writes, April 14, 1759, that "we must insist on the terms of the Deed and to the Day and a Half's Walk is not above forty-five miles, which surely is moderate walking." Having had the map of Benjamin Eastburn in his possession which states the Walk to be "about sixty miles," this he must have known was a falshood. If he meant the Blue Mountains to be the northern limits, John Chapman, by his survey, makes them forty-eight and three-quarter miles distant, and Eastburn, by his scale, forty-nine miles. Forty-five miles would certainly be moderate walking if they had not gone any further.

Timothy Smith, in his affirmation, made before Governor Denny, March 15, 1757, states "that previous to going the said walk he was requested by the said James Steel by order of the said Proprietor to acquaint the Persons who were to perform the walk that he was desirous they should not overwalk themselves, that he was not anxious or coveted to have so much land beyond ——— mountains, as that it should occasion their hurting themselves." There is something suspicious in this blank. Our opinion is that Timothy Smith gave the name of this mountain, and that Thomas Penn, in his papers before the king and government, from policy, had it expunged, so as to appear as if it had always been so. It is our belief that Thomas Penn was not present at either of the Walks, as would appear too by the correspondence relating to it. The city had too many attractions for one of his tastes, and it was only during the summer heats that he would leave it for the country.

It must follow, where documents relating to any subject are kept concealed and access prohibited, that many errors must occur, particularly in the case of this Walk, where after the matter had lain dormant for nearly twenty years it was suddenly brought into notice by the complaint of the Indians and, to their honor, the Society of Friends, in part through the wrongs perpetrated in this affair. These errors have been so numerous, that we shall only pretend to notice a few. John Watson, Sr., says the walk was made the 12th of September, 1735, and occupied but one day. We find a number of writers say that the walk was eighty-six miles, based on Moses Marshall's statement. That Yates got blind and died three days afterwards from the effects of the walk, and that Jennings had so injured his health as to have lived but a few years. This was published by Samuel Preston. The fact is, Yates was living in 1750, and Jennings till 1757. Biographical sketches of both these individuals will be found in another chapter. The Walk was not made through the Blue Mountains at either Smith's Gap or the Wind Gap, but at the Lehigh Gap. In both Day's Historical Collections and Armor's Lives of the Governors of Pennsylvania, the Walk is stated to have been in September, 1733. There is no evidence of any walk having taken place in that year. The Trial Walk came off privately as stated, in the spring of 1735, and has been mistaken for the Walk of 1737. The witnesses agree that the distance was

OBSERVATIONS ON THE WALK. 111

travelled from Wrightstown to Durham creek, in six hours, which may be fairly estimated at thirty miles, averaging five miles per hour, which may well be regarded as most extraordinary walking.

CHAPTER IX.

RESULTS OF THE WALK.

The writer has pretty freely expressed his opinion in the foregoing chapters regarding the conduct of the Penns in their intercourse with the Indians and colonists, which is regretted as anything but favorable, and what follows will be but little to their advantage. Truth and candor compel us to say this; and he who will overlook or gloss errors is not fitted for the duties of an impartial historian. Reviling is unpleasant, overrating is flattery, but vindicating the rights of the weak and the ignorant is noble. The oppressor, by virtue of his power, for the general good, needs a bringing down, and the degraded to be upheld and elevated; the effect is a moral improvement in both. It is a law of nature that there shall be a regular series of vegetable changes for the general well being; so in the human race that families shall have their successive chances to rise and dwindle away. The Penn family has had its day, and in name now no longer exists. Here the two parties contended, but in a century they disappeared together. One withdrew slowly to the west and the other to a more congenial home across the broad Atlantic; while in the place of both the despised colonists have now become the citizens of a mighty republic.

To prove that we have not been prejudiced in our views, we now propose to give extracts showing the opinions of various writers as to the results of the Walk. "The farthest point," remarks A. B. Burrell, in his Reminiscences of George La Bar, "that the Indians had supposed the walk to extend had been passed three hours before. They began to murmur at the cheat, and when Marshall started the next morning he had to go alone. The country north of the Forks was the Indians' favorite ground. They feared it would now be lost; the whites wanted to reach around the Minisink. Taking advantage of the curve, it was declared that the line strike the river at Lackawaxen. Thus the Minisink was swooped into the Penn colony. From the point where Marshall ended his walk it took *four days to reach the river.* Had they aimed for the nearest point, they would have reached it at the Water Gap in less than a day. But then it would not have taken in the coveted prize. The great Indian Walk, which took place just twenty-six years before 1763, was the first great source of contention and bloodshed to the settlers of the Forks region. Previous to that Walk the settlers of Penn's Colony had dwelt together in peace with the Indians. The kindness of Penn created a corresponding spirit in them which lasted through many years; but after the father of the colony was gone, the white man's treachery revealed itself, stirred up the savage nature of the red man, and many an innocent mother and child paid the penalty with their lives."

"Most of the Assembly," says Samuel Preston, "and many other judicious persons thought the whole affair a species of gambling worse than horse racing, and threatened the peace of the country. No further steps were taken in the matter, and Thomas Penn, seeing how his views and measures were treated, returned to England. This may be the reason why Robert Proud has omitted the whole transaction, as also the two treaties held in Easton in 1756 and 1758, and which were most important in the history of those times." "The name of William Penn," remarks Mr. Armor in his Lives of the Governors of Pennsylvania, "has by some persons been unjustly coupled with this disgraceful transaction, which did not take place till many years after his death. The Indians felt themselves much aggrieved by this unfair admeasurement of their lands; it was the cause of the first dissatisfaction between the Indians and the people of Pennsylvania; and it is remarkable that the first murder committed by them in the province, seventy-two years after the landing of Penn, was on this very ground which had been taken from them by fraud."

"During the administration of Governor Thomas in 1742," says Mr. Gordon in his History of Pennsylvania, "a convention of deputies from the Six Nations and Delaware Indians, was held at Philadelphia, for the purpose of terminating some dispute which had arisen between the latter tribe and the proprietaries, relative to a cession of lands. A tract, lying in the forks of the Delaware and Lehigh rivers, extending back into the woods *as far as a man can go in a day and a half,* denominated the *walking purchase,* had been sold by the Delawares in 1736 and confirmed by the same tribe by their deed, dated 25th of August, 1737. The lines of this purchase having been traced by very expert walkers, and including more land than the Indians expected, increased the dissatisfaction which had prevailed among them in relation to the grant of 1736. The Indians complained that the walkers, who outstripped them, ran, and did not pursue the course of the river, as they anticipated. The chief Nutimus and others, who signed the treaty of 1737, refused to yield peaceable possession of these lands, and declared their intention to maintain themselves by force of arms. Under these circumstances, the proprietaries invoked the interposition of the Six Nations, whose authority over the Delawares was well known. Upon this invitation, a deputation of 230 from these powerful tribes visited Philadelphia where they were met by delegates from the Delawares, who had also been invited."

"The northwest boundary," says John Watson, Sr., in his account of the Walk, "was afterwards run on the Pocono, and to the river at the short bend, and down the courses of the Delaware, by a measurement then made more than one-hundred miles to the spruce tree. This scandalous transaction was the subject of much conversation, and an apprehension prevailed that it would some time produce serious consequences. Surveyors were sent for six years successively to locate large tracts of land in the Forks, even among the Indian towns. They therefore procured letters to be sent to Jeremiah Langhorne and the governor, advising to remove the settlers or they would take up the hatchet against them, and the affair was now become serious, and therefore a deep laid scheme was contrived and carried into execution." "It appears," says Charles B. Trego, in his Relation of the Walk, "from the written statements of persons who were present as well as from various traditionary accounts of the proceedings connected with it, that there was a studied intention, and a preconcerted scheme on the part of the proprietary agents, to extend the walk as far as possible in the most favorable direction; and that a line was drawn from its termination by such a course to the river as should include within the limits of the survey all the desirable land in the forks of Delaware, and along the river above the Blue Mountain."

"The Indians did not value," says M. S. Henry, in his History of the Lehigh Valley, "the lands south of the Blue Mountains very highly; their favorite hunting grounds at that time were in the Minisink country, or the valley north of that mountain, extending from the Wind Gap into the state of New York, near the Hudson River; and as a rectangular line was drawn from the terminating point of the walk to the Delaware River, many miles northward of the Minisinks were included in the purchase, as well as their favorite hunting-grounds along that river, a result which was contrary to their expectations, and which caused them

to be much dissatisfied, and eventually, through the agency of some of the enemies of the proprietaries, became exasperated ; the consequence of which was that they committed many murders, and finally became involved in a war with the whites from 1755 to 1758."
"Public notice having been previously given," says Day in his Historical Collections, "in the papers, the famous Indian Walk was performed by Edward Marshall. This walk was the cause of jealousies and heartburnings among the Indians, that eventually broke out in loud complaints of injustice, and atrocious acts of savage vengeance." "The unfairness practiced in the walk," says Thomas Furniss, who was present, "both in regard to the way, where, and the manner how, it was performed, and the dissatisfaction of the Indians concerning it, were common subjects of conversation in our neighborhood, for some considerable time after it was done." "As we have observed," remarks Drake in his Book of the Indians, "the end of these affairs was war. The Delawares were driven back, and they joined the French against the English."

"When they arrived at the Blue Mountain," as Moses Marshall informed John Watson, Jr., in 1822, "they found a great number of Indians collected expecting the walk would there end, but when they found it was to go half a day further they were very angry, and said they were cheated. Penn had got all their good land, but that in the spring every Indian was to bring a buckskin and they would have their land again, and Penn might go to the devil with his poor land. An old Indian said 'no sit down to smoke, no shoot a squirrel, but lun, lun, lun all day long.' He says his father never received any reward for the walk, although the governor frequently promised to have the five hundred acres of land run out for him, and to which he was justly entitled. His father said the Indians always insisted that the walk should have been up the river, along the nearest path, which was also his opinion, and that they had been improperly dealt with, and cheated out of their land, but would have quietly submitted if the walk had not extended beyond the Blue Mountain."

"Having reached the farthest possible point," remarks Dr. Charles W. Smith in his History of Wrightstown, "to the north-westward, it now remained to draw a line from the end of the Walk to the river Delaware. The course of this line not being described in the Deed of Purchase, the agent of the Proprietaries, instead of running by the nearest course to the river, ran northeastward across the country, so as to strike the Delaware near the mouth of the Lackawaxen—thus extending far up the river, taking in all the Minisink territory, and many thousand acres more than if they had run by the nearest course to the Delaware. It is well known that the Delaware Indians immediately saw and complained of the manner in which these things were done, as a fraud upon them; nor would they relinquish the land until compelled to do so by the deputies of the Six Nations, at the treaty of 1742. The proceedings at this walk are mentioned as one of the causes of the hostile feelings of the Indians, which eventually led to war and bloodshed; and the *first* murder committed by them in the Province was on the very land they believed themselves cheated out of. The Indians always contended that the Walk should be up the river by the nearest path, as was done in the first day and a half's walk by William Penn; and not by the compass, across the country, as was done in this case. It is said that afterwards, when the surveyor general, and other persons to assist him, passed over this ground, it employed them about four days to walk to the extent of the purchase."

"This walk extended, it is said (Smith's Laws of Penna. Vol. II, pp. 116–17), about thirty miles over the Kittatinny Mountain; and a draught of it was made by Surveyor General Eastburn, including the best of the lands in the forks of Delaware and the Minisinks. The walkers were experts, and the Indians who could not keep up with them complained that they ran; and moreover it would appear that their expectation was that the walk was to be made up the river, by its courses. It is not intended to enter further into the controversy than to exhibit the general grounds which are said to have estranged the Delawares from our interest, and drove them into that of the French, who were always ready, in those times, to increase their dissatisfaction with the English. Nutimus and others who signed the release of 1737 were not willing to quit the lands nor give quiet possession to the people who came to take up lands and settle in the forks. They remonstrated freely, and declared their resolution of maintaining possession by force of arms."

Thomas Penn, in a letter supposed to be addressed to Isaac Norris, dated Braywick, July 1, 1755, says: "I am greatly concerned to find such a spirit of discontent gone forth in Pennsylvania against us and our government, as I think we have not given any just cause for it. However, I hope the people themselves will soon be convinced they have been most grossly imposed upon." Judge Langhorne, under date of May 20, 1737, not two years after the Trial Walk, thus writes to John Penn, in England: "It is very plain to me that there are a set of people about Philadelphia that have no good liking to the government under your family, but could they have their desires have it under the crown." In a letter to Thomas Penn, by the Rev. Richard Peters, dated Philadelphia, December 11, 1756, is this extract: "Be assured that the bulk, nay seven-eighths of the Society of Friends, are determinately your enemies. They do say, and will publish in England, and will assure the ministry, that the Delawares would have never taken up the hatchet against the Province, if the Proprietors had done the Indians justice—that Mr. Thomas Penn knew they complained of that scandalous Walk, and instead of pacifying them, set their Uncles the Six Nations against them, and they have been at variance ever since to the great injury of the British interest, and the particular damage of this Province. I hope the Proprietors will not fail to consider whether it may not be proper to offer them a present to take off their particular complaint, as to the land of the Forks."

CHAPTER X.

WHAT BROUGHT FORTH THE DOCUMENTS.

Benjamin Franklin, as agent appointed by the Assembly for Pennsylvania, referred his petition to the Committee of the Board of Trade and Plantations in London, Feb. 2, 1759, and which was addressed "To the King's Most Excellent Majesty." Among a number of charges relating to the conduct of the proprietaries, mention was made therein "That at some of their conferences, particularly at one holden at Easton, in Pennsylvania, the 13th of November, 1756, Teedyuscung complained that the Indians had been unjustly dispossessed and defrauded of large quantities of Land, by your Majesty's subjects, particularly of the Lands which are included within the Forks of the River Delaware, and also of other lands, on both sides of said River. That, at another conference holden at Easton in July, 1757, Tedyuscung having earnestly desired that all differences between the Indians and your Majesty's subjects might be referred to your Majesty's Royal Determination, and that the same might be published throughout all Your Majesty's Provinces, it was finally agreed (among other things) by the said George Croghan, the said Lieutenant Governor and Tedyuscung, that all the Purchase Deeds and Writings, by which the said Thomas and Richard Penn, or their ancestors, or the grantees of their Ancestors, now hold any Lands, within the back Parts of the Province of Pennsylvania, should be examined, and copies thereof laid before your Majesty, for Your Royal Decision, of the Bounds and Limits, between the Lands heretofore bought of the Indians and those yet unpurchased."

This accounts for the cause that led to the inquiry and origin of the documents relating to the Indian Walk and its results. This, it will be seen, was about twenty years after that occurrence, when it had almost been forgotten, and thus suddenly and unexpectedly revived with increased interest. Little did that crowd think that assembled around the chestnut tree in Wrightstown at sunrise on the morning of September 19, 1737, to see the walkers start, that the proceedings of that and the following day would thus some time afterwards produce the excitement it did and be laid before the King, and in which some of the prominent characters of the age should figure.

In behalf of Thomas and Richard Penn, their lieutenant governor, William Denny, held a meeting in Philadelphia, December 14, 1756, in which he "recommended it to Council to make Enquiry into the state of the Proprietary Indian purchases, and particularly of such as were made of any Lands comprised within the bounds mentioned by Teedyuscung, in his speeches at Easton, and to examine the Council Journals, and all other Books, Papers and Evidences relating to the late and former transactions with the Indians, and particularly the Evidences who were present at the one and half day's Walk, performed in pursuance of the Deed of 1686, and Confirmation Deed in 1737, and every thing else that may give light into this Affair, that he might be furnished in Time with all necessary Informations and Materials to enable him to make a proper Defence for the Proprietaries and government against the Charges made by Teedyuscung at the late Treaty. All the Members of Council promise to give their Assistance in and to meet as often as called upon to Expedite the Enquiry; but the care thereof is more immediately committed to Mr. Hamilton, Mr. Shoemaker and Mr. Logan, and the secretary is ordered to furnish and lay before the Committee all the Proprietaries' Deeds for the Indian purchases, together with the Council Books, Minutes of Property, Indian Treaties, and every other matter necessary for the said Enquiry." This was about the first step taken by the proprietary side towards their defence, brought about by the Treaty held at Easton with the Indians, November 8th, previous. Governor Denny now exerted his utmost for his employers, and accordingly issued his summons to witnesses present at the Walk. Nicholas Scull's deposition was taken January 25, 1757, Edward Marshall's, March 2; Alexander Brown's, March 5; Timothy Smith's, March 15; John Heider's, March 21; and Ephraim Goodwin's, August 3, of said year. Four of these were then residents of Bucks county.

At a council held March 29, 1757, "The Governor enquired of Mr. Logan, what Progress was made by the Committee in their examination of the Charges made by the Indians at Easton, against the Proprietors, and was told by him that all the Indian Deeds were read over, the Minutes of Council extracted and the Witnesses examined who were present at the day and half's Walk, but it was difficult to get a Meeting of the Committee, and more of the Council might be added to it." Several months afterwards we find additional information in the Minutes of the Council in relation to the aforesaid: "That a long time elapsing and nothing done, it was mentioned at the next Council held after the Treaty at Easton, in July and August, 1757, and the uneasiness the Governor was under at this delay, appearing very great, he then repeatedly afterwards desired all the Members would give their attendance and go through with it, and that accordingly the Members frequently met at the secretary's, Mr. Shoemaker being sometimes present, and the Indian Deeds and other Papers relative thereto were read and examined, and abundance of conversation passed; but coming to no conclusion, and more time still elapsing, a report was drawn up by the other Members and the Council regularly summoned in order to have the same read; and it was accordingly very carefully read in Council, examined and approved."

William Peters, in a letter from Philadelphia, of October 19, to Thomas Penn, thus expresses himself on the subject: "My Brother and the Committee of Council for inquiring into and answering the Indian or rather Quakers' heavy charge against you at Easton, November 8, 1756, having soon after that Treaty desired me to take Depositions of the Witnesses about the one and a half day's Walk in 1737 and undertake the drafting of the Report, &c. I endeavored to make myself master of the Affair by perusing all the Indian Deeds, Minutes of Council and ancient papers; and draw up a Draft, but it was laid aside for some time. But on Mr. Hamilton's proposing to go to England, it being thought necessary that some kind of Answer to that Charge should be settled to take with him, I prevailed on that gentlemam that no way of doing it could be so effectual as by Report of a Committee of the Council purposely appointed and to introduce all the Proofs in a schedule, and not by way of loose Ex Parte Affidavits, and then send home a copy under the sanction of the great Seal and having your Approbation and being an Act of the Governor and Council, supporting it with such ample proofs as would fully answer and confute all that vile charge against you to obtain a Decree in Chancery to establish a good title on the ancient copy of the Deed of 1686. From that Deed being lost and the old Copy produced in lieu of it, I presume these wicked people found that base charge of Forgery and your cheating the Indians of their land, and expect to establish their grand scheme of throwing the odium of the Indian ravages on you, as being the consequence of the Indians' Dissatisfaction and Resentment for which your iniquitous treatment of them as those vile Enemies of yours would have it believed and imputed, and not to the true cause, their refusing to give those Indians the hatchet and to protect and join with them against the French when they so warmly and repeatedly solicited us, particularly Scarroyady addressed to Governor Morris and the Assembly in August, 1755; and when if they had in earnest struck in with and made a proper use of those Indians,—a great part of those fatal mischiefs, which immediately followed, might have been prevented. The Committee have had my draught of the Report under consideration sometime and understand some of them think it too long; but in an affair of such consequence and which so much affects your Honour and Interest I thought I could not be too full; and I hope we shall prevail on them to sign it and then send you a copy by Mr. Hamilton."

As just stated the report of council was duly prepared on the Indian complaints and signed by five of its members, two dissenting. We propose to give a few more extracts therefrom to show its contracted and illiberal views, and which is by no means truthful. It is just what might be expected from the circumstances under which it was produced. The Governor was yet the faithful servant of the one who gave him the position, though he never furnished him a penny in the way of compensation, and a majority of the council was but a packed body controlled by the said Governor and Richard Peters, the secretary who acted under instructions from Thomas Penn, as we find by his correspondence and how he had his every wish obeyed.

For their services Lynford Lardner and Benjamin Chew were both well rewarded by official positions. As to John Mifflin, Joseph Turner and Thomas Cadwallader we are at present unable to say much. The report was addressed to Governor Denny, and was approved and signed January 6, 1758.

It commences by stating that "agreeably to the order of Council, appointing us a Committee to enquire into the pretended causes assigned by the Indians at the said Treaty for their striking the English, and destroying so many of our back inhabitants, and their complaints of injustice said to be done them by the Proprietaries in some of their Indian Purchases, we have carefully looked into and considered the same, and also the Proprietaries' Deeds for their several Indian Purchases, from the first settlement of the Province down to this time, with other, the instruments, books, papers and evidences which could furnish us with any lights into the affair. That instead of (the walkers) beginning at Wrightstown and going back into the woods a north-westerly course, as they did, they should have gone along by the courses of the river Delaware or the nearest path to it; that they walked too fast, and should not have kept walking constantly, but have frequently stopped to smoke a pipe, &c., and that the length of the walk was unreasonable and extravagant. In answer to which objections, we beg leave to observe, that in the month next after the date of the said Confirmation Deed, and in pursuance of the Agreement therein specified, the said One and a Half Day's walk was regularly performed in the presence of Mr. Eastburn, the then surveyor general, since deceased; Mr. Timothy Smith, the then high sheriff of Bucks county, in which those lands lay, who were appointed, by and on the part of the Proprietaries, to superintend and see the same fairly performed, with Mr. Scull and divers other persons, and of some Delaware Indians appointed by their chiefs for that purpose; and after the same had been fairly performed, as set forth in the hereto annexed affidavits of Edward Marshall, the survivor of the walkers, Mr. Scull, the present surveyor general, the said Mr. Smith, and several others present thereat.

"The said Mr. Eastburn laid down the tract, course, beginning and end of the said Walk in a fair Map which he drew of the contiguous lands, &c., in order to ascertain and complete the extent and description of the said disputed Lands, in the parts for which Blanks had been left, until the one and half day's journey or Walk should be performed, and that the said map was accordingly lodged and is now found with the proprietaries' Indian Deeds, as mentioned in the heretofore annexed affidavits. And then as the Deed requires that the head or cross line shall go directly from the end of the said south westerly side line and of the Walk to the River Delaware in one line or course, as we understand it, we cannot but think as Mr. Eastburn did, that it is most rational and equitable that the said Head or Cross line should run at right angles from the course of the walk and end of the south westerly side line. And it was not to be such a walk, but a real Day and Half's journey on an affair of so much consequence as the settling the boundaries of so large a purchase, and considering that according to the natural construction of those words (a journey as far as a man can go in a Day and a Half), the walkers were not strictly to be confined to walking, though by the affidavits of the said persons present it appears they did. We think the length of the Walk (especially stopping at the Kittatinny Mountains, where, according to Mr. Thomas Penn's directions, as mentioned in Mr. Smith's deposition, and where by the said purchase in 1749, that head line was fixed as aforesaid), it being only, as we are well informed, about forty-seven miles from Wrightstown to those mountains, was not at all extravagant or unreasonable and ought not to have been objected to. We don't find that any of the Proprietary Indian Purchases were ever run out by a compass, nor can we apprehend that it could be of any use in laying them out, as they seem all to be described in the Deeds by natural bounds; and therefore we are very much at a loss to understand what Tedyuscung means by that part of his charge against the Proprietaries, wherein he complains 'that when he (meaning, we suppose, the ancestors of the present Delaware Indians) had agreed to sell the land to the old Proprietary by the course of the River, the young Proprietaries came and got it run out by a straight line by the compass, and by that means took in double the quantity intended to be sold.'"

The report further states that they cannot understand that there were any grounds for a charge of forgery against the proprietaries except in offering the copy of the deed of 1686. They confess that no original could be produced; but they offer no apology for its not having been recorded or that it was rendered obsolete by the purchase of 1718. About the Trial Walk, of Allen's purchases, and others, nothing is said, or why anything relating to the Walk was withheld from public inspection, except such as they permitted. They profess great ignorance about the use of the compass in this transaction. Its advantage was in the use made with it by John Chapman in laying out the most direct route through the woods for the Trial Walk, and at the close of the Walk of 1737, so that it should run exactly southwest, that the northeast line at a right angle should strike the Delaware near the mouth of the Lackawaxen, thus taking in double the quantity of land it otherwise should, and which on a map is quite apparent. They further say that those witnesses are the most worthy of credit who mention that the Indians expressed *no dissatisfaction* about the Walk. Though Benjamin Eastburn's map is mentioned, of which it appears they had the use, nothing is said of the distance thereon "*of about sixty miles.*"

We now approach an interesting subject, the effort made by Thomas Penn, through his agents, to entrap William Logan and Benjamin Shoemaker of the Council, without their knowledge, into his infamous schemes.

The plot was pretty ingenious and such as we might expect from one who but a few years before had displayed such extraordinary skill in getting possession of the present Franklin Square, under the design of pretended benevolence. In this affair it is regretted that all our information comes from the proprietary side and therefore the more favorable. In the Colonial Records (Vol. VIII., p. 245) we learn that Mr. Logan and Mr. Shoemaker, having perused the Report of Council which lay on the table, declared that it was a transaction utterly unknown to them, and that the secretary had never given them notice that such a report was drawn. That they had further been told by some Friends, that a report was sent by the Governor to the Proprietary, in which their Society was abused ; and that a copy of it had been produced from London ; that their characters suffered on this account, it being known that they were of the committee appointed to inquire into the causes of the complaint and charge of forgery made by Tedyuscung at the Treaty of Easton in November, 1756, and therefore desired that their ignorance of this transaction might be entered, which was agreed to. They were further desired to give their own sentiments and account of it, in order that they might be inserted in the minutes.

To cover this affair, Thomas Penn sent a letter to William Logan, dated London, April 14, 1759, in which he says: "I had sent me a Report of some Members of Council, which I thought you must have seen, as you wrote me long since that you did not agree to every part of the Report that was then drawing, and at the same time sent me your narrative of the proceedings on this purchase." Some time previous to the above, Richard Hockley had sent a letter to the proprietary in which he says: "As I was instrumental in renewing correspondence between you and Mr. Logan, I think it my duty to offer some thought on that subject for your consideration. Mr. Logan is a very honest man, has the character, and I believe is so, as well attached to your family, but his connections and attachment to Friends is so manifest that I am apprehensive he cannot be of that service as I could wish; he will draw a veil over their most glaring mistakes."

From Thomas Penn's correspondence we are enabled to furnish some additional information respecting William Logan and this affair. He writes to Richard Peters, April 12, 1759: "I am very sorry you have had so much trouble about the Report of the Council, and am as certain as I can be of anything they had not their Copy from mine, as it has caused a difference betweeen the Members much to be regretted. Mr. Logan mentions it to me, and says its being kept secret from him, was from a subscription, that now the other Members of Council are satisfied was without foundation, so that I hope he will not think more about it. I am concerned in particular for your situation, but hope Mr. Logan will not long continue his resentment, as he knows the reason for it. I desire you will inform the gentlemen, that the Friends could not have the information from my Copy unless it was opened at the Post Office." Under date of Stoke, August 7, 1764, to Governor John Penn, he says: "As to Mr. Logan I expect nothing good from him, but wish you would show civility to him unless he gives you personal cause to alter your conduct in that respect, as his family have been so long concerned in our affairs, tho' I have had great objections to his Father's conduct on some occasions. I did not think, however, he would have abetted openly the signing the petition to the King." To Governor Hamilton, October 9, 1761, he wrote: "I am much concerned to hear Israel Pemberton still acts so bad a part and think he should be well watched to see whether he makes himself liable to be prosecuted for scandal either against us or those we have employed, or else for misdemeanor in case he acts any part that may tend to alienate the Indians from the rest of his Majesty's subjects, or cause them to distrust those employed in the Government of his provinces."

We would say that in the minutes of Council no papers whatsoever are to be found respecting the dissent of William Logan and Benjamin Shoemaker to the Report which had been endeavored to be imposed upon them. That there must have been such we think the aforesaid sufficiently reveals, but like other papers through the proprietary orders must have been either abstracted or destroyed. The whole was a gross outrage of which the most prominent actors were Thomas Penn, Governor Denny, Richard Peters,

Richard Hockley and perhaps Benjamin Chew. It was very important in this Report for Thomas Penn in his defence before the King to quiet and smooth over these transactions, and at the same time secure the influence of William Logan and Benjamin Shoemaker and have them in opposition to his leading opposers, who were also Friends, and thus have them divided, but in which he was completely foiled. The result was a letter from Thomas Penn, dated London, March 11, 1763, and addressed to Lieutenant Governor James Hamilton, in which he says: "Mr. Logan has sent me a most insolent letter, of which I shall send you a copy by the next Packet. You speaking to him I thank you for, and am of opinion that he has not acted a fair part in his professions to me." That "most insolent letter," could it be found, would no doubt throw much additional light on the subject and supply considerable which is now wanting. Such missives to him, however, were not infrequent.

The true representatives of the people, we mean the members of Assembly, also became interested in the affairs that were now agitating, and in their proceedings we find that on the 12th of July, 1757: "In obedience to an order of the House we made application to Richard Peters, Esq., Clerk of Council, and requested that he would permit us to inspect the minutes of Council, and furnish us with a fair transcript of such Minutes as related to Indian affairs; but he informing us, that he could not grant our Request without consulting the Governor, and receiving the said Request in writing, we wrote him the following letter:

Sir, The Application of the Committee of Assembly to you yesterday, was made in pursuance of an Order of the House, which was to inspect the Minutes of Council, respecting Indian Purchases. They are desirous of seeing and having fair transcripts of all the Minutes that relate to the Purchase made by William Penn about the year 1700, of the Lands on Tohiccon, Neshaminy, the Lehigh, and the Forks of Delaware, or any of them. The Minutes relating to the confirmatory Purchase of the same Lands in 1737: The Minutes relating to the Purchase of the Lands on Brandywine: The Minutes relating to the Purchase of the Juniata and Conedaquinet Lands; and those relating to the Purchase made at Albany. We are, sir, your humble servants.

      JOSEPH FOX,
      THOMAS LEECH,
      JOSEPH GALLOWAY,
      WILLIAM MASTERS,
      WILLIAM WEST,
      THOMAS YORKE.

And the next day we received for answer the following letter from the secretary, viz.:

Gentlemen, I have laid before his Honor the Governor your Application for an inspection and fair transcripts of the Minutes of Council, respecting the several Indian Purchases mentioned in your letter of this date. In answer to which his Honor has ordered me to let you know, That he will not permit you to inspect the Council Books. That he is now too much engaged in public business, and in preparing for his journey to Easton, to admit of time for my searching the Council Books for the Minutes you apply for; but that on his return he will take care you shall be furnished with fair transcripts of them. This, he presumes, will not be attended with any inconvenience to you as a Committee of Assembly, as the house does not meet by their adjournment till the 8th day of August next. I am, Gentlemen, your most humble servant.

RICHARD PETERS.

"Since which," the said Committee of Assembly reports, "we have never heard from, or received any of, said Minutes, either from his honour the Governor, or the said clerk."

This was on the 28th of September following and immediately on their adjournment. So it will be seen that these efforts met with as little success as the Friendly Association. Who on reading such high-handed proceedings will not rejoice at the triumph of the Revolution that overthrew this corruption—the growth of nearly a century?

CHAPTER XI.

THE PROPRIETARIES AND THE SOCIETY OF FRIENDS.

The many wrongs practiced by the proprietaries in the government of their colony, particularly on the Indians, originated in part in the Walk, and it comes within the scope of the present work to set this matter in a true light. The consequences have been actually attributed "to the Quakers," and we have seen it so published both here and abroad. This statement, from its novelty, would to many residing in the southeastern section of Pennsylvania appear absurd because unfounded. Not so, however, with many outside of these limits, as, for instance, in New England and among the descendants of the Connecticut settlers in the more northern portion of the State, who, if we are to believe what has been lately said in some of their accounts, have been in times past a dangerous people to those who were so unfortunate as to come within their power Now we mean to prove that the aforesaid opinion is incorrect, and that the Society of Friends, as a body, did nobly stand by the Indians, in the various wrongs that were inflicted on them, not by empty words and actions, but by the better Christian example of extraordinary acts of disinterested benevolence and friendship, which it is not likely was shown to an equal extent in any of the other English colonies. The erroneous ideas to which we have alluded, had their origin in the misconception that Penn and Quaker were synonymous or identical.

Gordon, in his History of Pennsylvania, makes the following remarks concerning the Society of Friends, and our own investigations lead us to concur in their truthfulness: "Their firm attachment to liberal political principles; their courage in resisting, by invincible moral force, every encroachment on the rights of conscience; their justice and kindness to the aborigines; their unostentatious but efficient charities, have all been noticed. If some inconsistencies between their principles and their practice are discovered, they prove only that our best resolutions are not always proof against the storms of passion or the wiles of expediency." At the commencement of the Indian troubles in 1755, the Society formed an organization called the Friendly Association, whose object was to redress the grievances of the Indians and preserve peace by more amicable relations between the parties. We have authority to show that between the years 1756 and 1765 £4523 provincial money was expended by the Association and distributed among the Indians, besides goods to the value of £815, from Friends in England. "I assure you," wrote Richard Peters to Thomas Penn, August 4, 1756, "if the Quakers had not been complying, and their large present to that provided by the Assembly, we should have been ruined, the Indians would have gone away dissatisfied, and matters made infinitely worse." The subscriptions were not exclusively confined to the Friends, for £430 of the amount named was contributed by the Mennonists, and other German sects. A large portion of the money was applied to the purchase of clothing and sundry articles of value to the Indians, which were presented either collectively at the treaties or on special occasions to individuals acting as interpreters, messengers, &c. We have in confirmation seen a receipt dated, Richland Monthly Meeting, Bucks county, 4 mo. 16, 1759, which informs us that there was "received of William Heacock, 12 shillings as one year's interest for £10, which he subscribed to ye Friendly Association for regaining and preserving peace with ye Indians," signed by Samuel Foulke as treasurer.

Besides this charity the Association went still further, for which they certainly deserve great credit, as it at once brought them in opposition to the proprietaries, and for which they had to suffer gross insults and slanderous charges. This was to examine into the justice of the claims made by the Indians for alleged abuses practiced on them for some time. This step was certainly one of the boldest mentioned in our colonial history, and for its moral execution required a degree of courage even greater than that often exhibited on the field of battle. It was in reality a political attempt to uphold the rights of the people and protect the weak and oppressed from the power of the strong. The sons of William Penn were here to be taught for the first time, and by this sect, that they were but men, and if scrupulously honest would in no respect fear investigation.

"Sorry I am," wrote Richard Peters, December 11, 1756, to Thomas Penn, "to see the vindictive spirit of the Quakers increase against the Proprietors, so contrary to faith plighted. Those who signed the address to you, were some of them deceived, and others deceivers; for, be assured that the bulk, nay seven-eighths of the Society, are *determinately* your enemies, and intend, in conjunction with Mr. Franklin and Mr. Norris and their dependents, to push against you with all the strength and fury they are able. They do say, and will publish in England, and will assure the ministry, that the Delawares would have never taken up the hatchet against this Province, if the Proprietors had done the Indians justice, that Mr. Thomas Penn knew they complained of that scandalous Walk, and instead of pacifying them set their Uncles the Six Nations against them, and they have been at variance ever since, to the great injury of the British interest and the particular damage of this Province."

The following is an extract of a letter dated Philadelphia, 21 of 1 mo., 1757, prepared in behalf of the Society of Friends, and addressed by William Callender and Israel Pemberton to Richard Peters, secretary of the Council: "An apprehension of difficulties which may probably arise between the Proprietaries and the Representatives of the People, in the adjusting of the Quotas of the Expenses which will attend a final Adjustment with the Indians, hath induced us to be prepared to contribute thereto, in order speedily to regain their Friendship, and that good understanding, which hath unhappily been interrupted, and as we find by the express terms of our original Deeds the Proprietaries are obliged to clear the Lands from all Titles, Claims or demands of the Natives, we apprehend we have a Right to be satisfied whether and how this has been done. And if we can at the next Treaty inform the Indians, that agreeably to their desire at the least, we have had full opportunity of searching into the Grounds of their claims, and that we find them under misapprehensions therein (which we have reason to believe is the case in some particulars), we are in hopes of being instrumental to engage them the more readily to comply with such measures as may then be proposed for an amicable settlement of all differences between them and this Government, which is what we sincerely desire."

In regard to the aforesaid matter, Mr. Peters thus expressed himself six days later to Thomas Penn: "Another troublesome application has happened since my last. The Quaker Association have taken it into their heads, that they have a right to search the Minutes of Council, and to inspect the Proprietary Deeds from the Indians, and Mr. Callender and Mr. Israel Pemberton were deputed to make the demand of me, as Provincial secretary, which they did verbally, but afterwards at my instance in writing, which is copied, together with my answer, dictated at the Council Board, and is one of Mr. Hamilton's draft. I hear the

Club of Friendly Associators have my answer under their consideration, and being refused the Examination will probably be made a charge against the Governor." In his reply, Thomas Penn stated that, "The refusal of suffering Mr. Pemberton and Mr. Callender to examine the Council Books was perfectly right and proper, and the letter of Mr. Hamilton's well known. If they apply to the Assembly and the Assembly demand to examine them, your answer should be the same; they have no right to examine Council Books, and therefore should be flatly refused. Let them make complaint, I am prepared to answer it."

At a Council held on the 25th, Mr. Hamilton and Mr. Mifflin laid before them a reply which was agreed to and delivered to the aforesaid by the secretary, who had signed it. As may be seen it is both arrogant and evasive: "I laid your Application in regard to the Inspection of the Council Books before his Honor the Governor, and in Answer thereto, I am commanded to acquaint you, that as those Books contain the most important Affairs of Government, many of which require the greatest secrecy, he cannot allow the perusal of them to any but those concerned in the Administration. And further, that he looks upon the transacting of Business with the Indians in this Province, to be a Matter so entirely pertaining to himself, that he cannot permit any but such as are immediately empowered by the King's Authority, or by his own, to treat with, or intermeddle in the affairs of that People. Nevertheless, if it be conceived that anything is contained in the Minutes of Council that does or may concern the Rights or Property of any Person whatsoever, such Person, by a proper Application, and by particularly pointing it out, may be furnished with a copy of it."

As a result soon after the Friendly Association prepared an Address to Governor Denny, in which they say, that "At the Governor's lodgings we first saw Tedyuscung, the Delaware chief, to whom we were before utterly strangers: on our coming in he immediately expressed his regard for and confidence in the Quakers" (this was in the hearing of Governor Morris, at Easton), and declared "He would not proceed to any business unless we were present; and confirmed it so evidently by his subsequent conduct, at that time, and the ensuing treaty, that we would not without unjustifiable neglect of our duty, decline contributing our utmost endeavors to improve this disposition to the interest of our country, so far as we might be able to do it, consistent with our respective stations in life. From that time it was generally known, that one cause of the alienation of that friendship was some injustice they had received, or supposed to be done them, in the purchases, and the running out of their lands. They complained of divers kinds of frauds, which had been committed, repeatedly urged, that an impartial inquiry should be made into the grounds of their complaints, by searching all our records, and by the strong motives of regard to our temporal and eternal interest, urged the Governor to give liberty to all persons and friends to search into those matters. Thus we thought ourselves under the strongest obligations to make all the inquiry in our power, into the true state of the Indian claims, whether or not such care had been taken to purchase, and pay them for the lands, as the Proprietaries' Agents had constantly asserted. The right of many of us who hold large tracts of land under the first settlers, the Governor's repeated declarations, both in public and in private, that those matters should be honestly and fully inquired into, and the Indians' injunctions that this should be done, not only by the persons thus complained of, or their Agents, but by others likewise interested therein, united in engaging our particular attention, and gave us a reasonable prospect of meeting with the Governor's approbation, and though the secretary refused to permit us to proceed therein, by inspecting the records in his office, we still had cause to think our farther application to the necessary and important concern of regaining peace, was not contrary to the Governor's inclination."

Thomas Penn, in a letter to Richard Peters, dated London, March 11, 1757, says: "The malice of the Quakers in assisting the Indians to make the charge is very visible, and I make no doubt will by you be discovered. You see in the General Instructions there is no mention made of the Walk, but the directions to remove any other pretense for complaint were meant with a particular view, to the dissatisfaction, which you in your letters say some of the Indians have expressed with respect to it." Again, under date of November

11, 1758, to the same: "Israel Pemberton's hints are very impertinent, and will not be the means of gaining for the Indians one shilling more from me that they would otherwise have. The Indians I think should be made sensible, that it is to their interest to preserve a good understanding with the governments, for these only give temporary presents, and it may be many years before they receive any presents again, and upon the same principle they should not assist our own people to be troublesome to government." To Governor Denny he writes, April 13, 1759: "Mr. Pemberton's behaviour at the Treaty at Easton, was void of all decency, and as you will observe must tend to distract all business. This intrusion of those people into Public business is under consideration and must if possible be prevented." This coming from one who was not only the son of William Penn, but had actually come here in 1732, with a Friend's certificate of removal, addressed to the Philadelphia Monthly Meeting, sounds oddly enough as may be seen on record, and shows only the more his lack of moral principle.

Richard Hockley, the receiver general, under date of Philadelphia, June 30, 1757, to Thomas Penn, says: "Many Quakers are gone up to the Treaty, at Easton, and I am the more rivetted in my opinion of their mischievous intentions to do you all the injury that they possibly can, notwithstanding their audacious professions to the contrary as a body politic. I wish the treaty may turn out to your satisfaction and the good of the Province, but cannot say I have such sanguine expectations as some others as I dread the worst that can happen. I firmly believe that some of them were wicked enough to inveigle Tedyuscung to say what he did about the purchase of Lands, and endeavor to throw an odium on you of the blackest dye, to cover if possible their mal-administration and abuse of power."

A committee of Council consisting of Joseph Turner, Lynford Lardner, Benjamin Chew, John Mifflin and Thomas Cadwallader, drew up a Report addressed to Governor Wm. Denny, on the Indian Complaints, purporting to be chiefly prepared from the proceedings of the Treaty, held at Easton, November 8, 1756, but was not approved and signed by them until January 6, 1758. The object of this Report of course was to screen the conduct of the proprietaries from the grave charges that had been made against them by the Indians, more especially Tedyuscung. It may be seen in full, in the Colonial Records (Vol. VIII., p. 254), but from its length we can only make such extracts as relate to our purpose. They thus allude to the Friendly Association and their motives: "To Tedyuscung's making that base Charge of Forgery against the Proprietors to the malicious suggestions and management of some wicked people, enemies to the Proprietaries, who had come to the knowledge of that circumstance of the said Deed being lost, and that there was nothing but a copy of it now to be found, which they would have it believed to be a forged one, being ignorant that the truth and fairness of the said copy would be so well proved; and perhaps it would not be unjust in us if we were to impute it to some of those busy forward people, who, in disregard of the express Injunctions of His Majesty's Ministers against it, and your Honor's repeated Notices thereof served on them, would nevertheless appear in such crowds at all the late Indian Treaties, and there shew themselves so busy and active in the management and support of the Indians in these complaints against the Proprietaries."

This Report concludes with the following scurrilous attack on the Friends: "But the people who have since that time appeared so indefatigably industrious to engross all the management of the Indians to themselves, were chiefly the same who made up a great majority of the Assembly at the time when the House from their avowed religious principles, or from what other motives they best knew, refused or declined to concur with the Governor in giving up the hatchets to and joining with those Indians against the enemy, and as they cannot but be conscious that they justly deserve and must have incurred great blame on that account, if the Indians should have given that for the reason of their joining with the French against us, we are better able to account for these people being so numerous at at all the late Indian Treaties, and upon all occasions so very forward and anxious to ingratiate themselves with the Indians; and for Tedyuscung's choosing to offer these imaginar yreasons for their quarrel with us, rather than the true one."

Thomas Penn's correspondence reveals the fact that the Report of Council was prepared according to his instructions, and as soon as signed was confidentially transmitted to him for his defense before the King and the Board of Trade. The Friends having received information of a slanderous attack made on them, very probably through William Logan or Benjamin Shoemaker of the council, on being requested to sign it were astonished at the nature of its contents, and of course very properly refused to do so, which afterwards led to a sharp controversy with Thomas Penn, as has been mentioned in the previous chapter. The result was the following correspondence :

To William Denny, Esquire, Lieutenant Governor of the Province of Pennsylvania, and the three Lower Counties of New Castle, Kent and Sussex, upon Delaware.

The Address of the Meeting for Sufferings of the People, called Quakers, for the said Province and New Jersey, met at Philadelphia 14 of 12 month, 1758, Respectfully sheweth : That we have been lately informed that a report of a Committee of thy Council, appointed to inquire into the Complaints of the Indians, at the Treaty of Easton, the 8 of November, 1756, hath been some Months past drawn up and laid before the Governor, and since transmitted to England, and that there are some Matters alleged therein, in which the Reputation and Interest of our religious Society are immediately concerned. We, therefore, request the Governor would be pleased to order a true copy thereof to be made out and communicated to us, in order that we may have an opportunity of perusing the same, and be more perfectly acquainted with the contents thereof. Signed in behalf and by appointment of our said Meeting.   JAMES PEMBERTON, Clk.

At a Council held at Philadelphia, Wednesday, January 10, 1759, present the Hon. Wm. Denny, Esq., Lieut. Governor and Lynford Lardner and John Mifflin, Esquires, the Address of the Meeting of Sufferings, presented the 14th of December last, was again considered, and a draught kept under advisement was amended and agreed to, in these words:

Gentlemen: After Tedyuscung had in the Treaty at Easton, publicly charged the Proprietaries of this Province, with defrauding them of their lands ,I desired the Council to examine into the State of the Indian Treaties, Purchases, and all other Transactions with them, for my own satisfaction; and they were kind enough to do it, and to make a Report to me of their Examinations, which fully convinced me of the Falsehood of the Charge. This Report I transmitted to the Proprietaries at London, together with Copies of the Deeds and other Papers referred to therein; and as this matter principally affects those Gentlemen, who are to make their defence against this Charge, before His Majesty, you will easily perceive that I cannot, consistent with my Trust, order you the Copy you desire. I can only say that there is not the least Reflection in it upon any Religious Society, and I conceive the meeting of Sufferings have nothing to do

with it. If they think otherwise, I refer them to the Proprietaries. And am, Gentlemen,
> Your Most Humble Servant,
> WILLIAM DENNY.

Now what must we think of the character of Governor Denny for veracity when he says, "I can only say that there is not the least reflection in it upon any Religious Society." Poor Denny! he little thought how soon aftwards he would have to refer himself to the proprietaries in his pecuniary distress. Their tender mercies he at last found out, and his reward was like Edward Marshall's, *but fair promises.* The Friends, however, renewed their application on the 13th of the following month, to have a copy of the Council's Report, so as to defend themselves from any base charges which they feared might be contained therein, and closed by saying: "We desire the Governor and Council may not be displeased with this Application, but may give it the most charitable construction, and grant this our reasonable request." This we believe was about the last of the matter, but it conclusively proves that the Society of Friends took a bold stand on the side of freedom, and were the staunchest friends of the Indians against the conduct of the proprietaries and their agents. We thus perceive that they have been erroneously charged with aiding and abetting the Penns at the very time when these respective parties were almost alone in opposition to each other, even to the end of the proprietary rule.

CHAPTER XII.

BIOGRAPHICAL SKETCHES OF PROMINENT PERSONS CONCERNED IN THE WALK.

THOMAS PENN.

The subject of this notice was the son of William Penn, by his second wife, Hannah Callowhill, who on his death in 1718 left six surviving children. The province of Pennsylvania he bequeathed to the three sons of this marriage, being John, Thomas and Richard; the first mentioned being the eldest, received a double portion. John was born here on his father's last visit, and returned in September, 1734, but went back the following year, in order to oppose Lord Baltimore respecting the boundary. He died unmarried in October, 1746, and by his will left all his part of the province, which consisted of two shares or half the whole, to Thomas, who thus became the owner of three-fourths, and with his youngest brother Richard now the sole proprietor.

Thomas Penn arrived here August 11, 1732, and like his elder brother received from the colonists and the Assembly those marks of respect regarded as due their stations and as the sons of the illustrious founder. Aided by special commissioners, he entered upon the adjustment of the boundary, according to articles of agreement made the previous 10th of May. New points of dispute, however, arose; the matter was again adjourned, and was not finally settled until 1761. On his arrival here he was in his thirty-second year, and exhibited in his conduct the occasional pranks and follies of youth. He was cold in his manners and distant in his intercourse with society, a general characteristic of the family, and consequently unpopular. A part of his time he spent in fox hunting with horses and hounds that he had specially imported from England, and at least a portion of the balance, with all his pretentions, in no very select company.

It is useless to mention certain of his habits, which John F. Watson in his Annals and Sherman Day have had the manliness to expose, and we will therefore mention other occurrences in his life deemed essential and sufficiently well supported to show off the man who was at the head of outraging the Indians, and a cause for entailing a long and bloody war and countless misery on the people of a colony over whom he ruled through a grant given his father by the King for the naval services of an ancestor.

In the Pennsylvania Archives (Vol. I., p. 546), we find that Thomas Penn in company with Roger Freame, Robert Charles and four others from Philadelphia, only two months after the Walk, went over to Newtown, Gloucester county, N. J., and on the affirmation of Joseph Mickle, a respectable member of the Society of Friends, did there "enter in a riotous manner his enclosures, did beat and maim him and forcibly enter his house and spoil his goods, and declared that he was afraid of further harm to be done by the above persons, therefore he prayed surety of the peace against them." James Hinkon, the magistrate, accordingly issued a warrant to the constable for the arrest of the parties. What further was done in the matter we are unable to say, but suppose, as in the crimes committed some time previously by William Penn, Jr., in Philadelphia, the matter was dropped, owing to the influence and power of the parties. Joseph Smith, who was born in 1753, in his account of the Walk, states that though the Indians had been so grossly wronged, they could scarcely believe the wickedness of the sons of Penn when represented to them by the whites.

Though Thomas Penn had the Walks of 1735 and 1737 carried out, we are inclined to believe that he was not present at either, but that they were done by his instructions, through deputies. His residence in Pennsylvania was exactly nine years, a sufficient length of time to have become tolerably familiar with the people and the province, and to have seen what their necessities were in the way of a good and wise government. As he returned in August, 1741, it must have been before this date that Samuel Preston relates that Edward Marshall had told him that shortly after the Walk he went to see Thomas Penn, in Bucks county, probably at Pennsbury, and demanded from him a warrant for the five hundred acres that had been promised him as the best walker, to be located at Allentown, in compensation for his services, and that the only satisfaction he got was an offer of £5 for the same, when, for this exhibition of his meanness, he became so provoked as to curse him and his "half wife" to their faces.

In 1751, when in his fiftieth year, he married Lady Juliana, fourth daughter of Thomas Fermer, first Earl of Pomfret. We have seen the original marriage settlement of the parties, and it appears by the numerous papers relating thereto, that they had quite a time till it was adjusted to the satisfaction of both; employing for the purpose some of the ablest lawyers in England. What is generally regarded as an affair of the heart, seems to have been a matter of money with a strong persistence that neither should overreach the other. For the old Earl seems to have been very cautious on this matter, as if he had not been altogether ignorant of the person he had to deal with. While this business was in progress, he met with a singular accident, that might have turned out seriously. On account probably of robbers that frequented the highways at this period, he had with him a pair of loaded pistols under the seat of his chaise, and when about twelve miles from Bath, one of them accidentally discharged, and wounded him so severely as to have cost him several months surgical treatment.

The character of the man may be very well arrived at by his correspondence. To attain any particular end he would approach the person with the most endearing epithets and flattery. This is particularly observable in a correspondence he opened with his hitherto neglected nephew, William Penn, with a view of getting the Pennsbury estate, in Bucks county, from him at his own price. The following is an extract from a reply dated Dublin, February 4, 1741: "Dear Uncle Thom., I received thine of the 7th January with no small surprise, because I see there an affirmation that Pennsbury contains no more than 4000 acres of land, which is contrary to thy own repeated declarations and to the survey sent me, both of them calling it 5000 acres, but I have as good an authority as either to produce, which is a letter of my grandfather's, that expressly says it is 7000 acres; indeed if I had no such letters I should think it hard, and I would think it is strange that the deposition of hearsay should swear me out of 1000 acres of my property."

The following from another of his kindred is a more serious charge, and is extracted from a letter of Dr. Franklin (Sparks' Works of Franklin, Vol. VII., pp. 227–28), dated London, May 9, 1761, to Edward Pennington, an eminent merchant of Philadelphia, whose ancestors were related to William Penn's first wife, who was Gulielma Maria, daughter of Sir William Springett:

"I enclose you a letter from your kinsman, Mr. Springett Penn, with whom I have no acquaintance, until lately, but have the pleasure to find him a very sensible, discreet young man, with excellent disposition, which makes me the more regret that the government as well as property of our province should pass out of that line. There has, by his account, been something very mysterious in the conduct of his uncle,

Thomas Penn, towards him. He was his guardian; instead of endeavoring to educate him at home under his eye in a manner becoming the elder branch of their house, he has from his infancy been endeavoring to get rid of him. He first proposed sending him to the East Indies. When that was declined, he had a scheme of sending him to Russia; but the young gentleman's mother absolutely refusing to let him go out of the kingdom, unless to Pennsylvania to be educated in the college there, he would by no means hear of his going hither, but bound him an apprentice to a country attorney, in an obscure part of Sussex, which after two years' stay, finding that he was taught nothing valuable, nor could see any company that might improve him, left, and returned to his mother, with whom he has been ever since, much neglected by his uncle, except lately that he has been a little civil, to get him to join in a power of attorney to W. Peters and R. Hockley, for the sale of some Philadelphia lots, of which he is told three undivided fourth parts belong to him. But he is not shown the right he has to them; nor has he any plan of their situation, by which he may be advised of their value; nor was he told, till lately, that he had any such right, which makes him suspect that he may have other rights that are concealed from him. He has refused to treat about it at present, as well as to sign the power of attorney, for the sale of the city lots; upon which his late guardian has brought an account against him, and demands a debt of 400£., which he urges him to pay, for that, as he says, he very much wants the money, which does not seem to look well. Not only the Land office may be searched for warrants and surveys to the young gentlemen's ancestors, but also the Record office for deeds of gift from the first proprietor, and other subsequent grants or conveyances."

James Parton, in his Life of Franklin, in speaking of Thomas and Richard Penn, remarks with considerable truth: "They were haughty and reserved, they evaded and quibbled. Such men offend by their very concessions and *disgust by their generosity*." In speaking further of their meanness he says: "But in the imposition of the trifling sum of 550£. a year as tax on their estates, all of which was to be expended in the defence of what the proprietaries had the ill taste to style, 'our province of Pennsylvania,' and 'our city of Philadelphia,' they resisted with a blind obstinacy that was only surpassed by the enlightened firmness of the Assembly in insisting upon it. During the first years of the French war, from 1754 to the end of 1758, the ravaged colony contributed to the king's service, in defending its own borders and aiding other colonies to strike at the common foe, the sum of 218,000£. sterling. Still the proprietaries would not be taxed."

In confirmation that even the generosity of Thomas Penn was insulting, the following instances will show: He donated by deed dated July 21, 1759, twenty-five hundred acres of land in the Manor of Perkasie, in Bucks county, in support of the college in Philadelphia, now better known as the University of Pennsylvania, but with this proviso: That should the institution fail the land was to revert to himself and heirs, and when the income from it should amount to 200£. per annum, they should educate, maintain, and clothe two persons of the nomination of the grantor or his heirs. In a previous letter sent to Richard Hockley, dated October 9, 1756, he says: "I have also agreed to give on my private account 50£ a year towards the salary of the Provost of the College, provided he is approved by me, to commence from Christmas, 1755." We presume, from the conditions imposed, the offer was not accepted.

In the address of Dr. George Wood on the Centennial Celebration of the founding of the Pennsylvania Hospital, delivered June 10, 1851, we get some additional information. After a charter had been granted and a sum of money voted by the Assembly and considerable subscribed for the purpose of erecting a building, application was made to Thomas and Richard Penn for a plot of ground on which to build, "so that all concerned in the Province might participate in the honor, merit and pleasure of so good a work." A suitable place was designated on the unappropriated portion of the square on the south side of Mulberry between Ninth and Tenth streets, being a part of the city in which the value of land had not increased for several years, and which was not likely to be occupied. But, instead, they transmitted to their Lieutenant Governor, James Hamilton, an instrument from themselves for a small lot of ground, lying on

the north side of Sassafras street, between Sixth and
Seventh streets, being a portion of the grounds now
known as Franklin Square; under the condition, however, that should there not be a constant succession of
contributors to meet and choose managers, the tract
of land thus conveyed should revert to them or their
heirs. Now as this with the adjoining grounds had a
long time before been granted by the founder, their
father, to the city for public uses, it could not be accepted under the instrument conveying it "without an
inplied acknowledgment on their part of the Proprietaries' right to the remainder of the grounds." The
managers therefore unanimously felt themselves con-
strained to decline the grant of the Proprietaries. De-
sparing now of any donation from the Penns, they
purchased the square on which it now stands, in December, 1754, for 500£, to which however ten years
afterwards they did grant an adjoining lot fronting on
Spruce street, of sixty feet in depth and an annuity of
40£. They thus offered to convey ground for which
they had not been asked and never even owned; having been granted to the city about seventy years previous.

There are other similar occurrences in the life of
Thomas Penn that will be found elsewhere in this
work, and to which from their connection they more
appropriately belong. Between him and Dr. Franklin
an old antipathy existed, perhaps originating from a bill
many years due for printing and stationery, which the
latter, losing all patience from his quibbling, compelled

him to pay. In a letter to Richard Peters, dated London, July 5, 1758, he says: "How Mr. Franklin looked I cannot tell, but my brother says like a malicious v—— as he always does; how from this time I will not have any conversation with him on any pretense." Again, to the same, under date of February 10, 1759: "He has just now presented a Petition to the King on the Delaware Indian Complaints, a copy of which I send you." This related to the Walk, and the conduct of the Penns in their intercourse with the Indians. June 13, 1764, he writes again respecting Franklin to Lieut. Gov. James Hamilton, in which he says, "we are not in fear of your mighty Goliath, whose schemes of government are not approved of here, and who may lose the government of a post office by grasping at that of a province." Could he have lived twenty years later he would have found himself in a rather humiliated condition; his province forever lost him, and his King and government compelled to acknowledge it, and his antagonist prominent in bringing it about and serving twice as its chief executive.

After six years of severe suffering, Thomas Penn died March 21, 1775, when he had completed his seventy-fourth year, about the age of his father, and was his last surviving child. He had a large family, but most of his children died young. A son John was the author of two volumes of poems, but of no striking original merit. Another son, Granville, in 1834, presented the two Indian portraits to the Historical Society. His widow survived until 1801.

For the loss of the province, considering the conduct of the proprietaries, the Legislature of Pennsylvania certainly exhibited liberality. The act was passed November 27, 1779, that abolished their hereditary powers and other extraordinary privileges. It states "that the sum of 130,000 pounds sterling ($577,778) be paid to the devisees and legatees of Thomas Penn and Richard Penn, late proprietaries of Pennsylvania respectively, and to the widow and relict of the said Thomas Penn, in such proportions as shall hereafter by the legislature be deemed equitable and just upon a full investigation of their respective claims. Provided that no part of the said sum be paid within less than one year after the termination of the present war with Great Britain; and that no more than 20,000 pounds sterling, nor less than 15,000 pounds sterling, shall be paid in any one year, until the whole sum be fully paid and discharged." It appears that they gladly accepted it, and in 1791 the State had paid the whole off with interest. For their losses the British Government allowed the family an annuity of £4000 to continue forever. Thus did Pennsylvania prove a fortunate venture to the founder's descendants.

If it were asked in the rule of almost a century, what beneficial works of enterprise the Penns had performed for the good of the people and Province, we think it would be rather difficult to answer, while, on the other hand, the abuse of power in the government, and their neglect and mismanagement of business, caused incalculable injury. In that long period, they constructed no useful public works, founded nor endowed no humane or benevolent institutions, organized no schools or colleges; made even no attempts to civilize, instruct or convert the native Indians, or ameliorate the condition of the negroes. However, with all these drawbacks, the Province flourished, and was bringing in immense revenues to those who would not be taxed, who cared not even to reside here nor do anything for it, and yet whose vast possessions were augmenting in wealth through the labors of the hardy and enterprising settlers.

In concluding this sketch we shall leave the Rev. Israel Acrelius (Hist. New Sweden, ed. 1874, p. 131) furnish a parting salute: "Thomas Penn came in 1733 to visit his country, and examine into its resources. But as he and his brother Richard had entirely fallen away from the Quaker connection, and he inquired more about the government than the upholding of Quakerism, he was met by his father's old friends with uncommon disesteem, and after six or seven years' intercourse with them, instead of any other token of honor, had a gallows erected for him on the side of the road along which he travelled."

WILLIAM ALLEN.

In his day, William Allen was one of the most influential men in Philadelphia, if not in the Province. He was the son of William Allen, an eminent merchant in the city, of whom Robert Proud speaks as "a considerable promoter of trade and a man of good character." He died in the summer of 1725, and left to his son a considerable fortune. Mr. Allen, with James Logan and ten others, in the spring of 1727, took up what was called the Durham tract on the river Delaware in Bucks county, and which they said contained by estimation six thousand acres, which on a division in 1773 was found to contain eight thousand five hundred and eleven acres. His operations were now extensive, and being a man of wealth, and the Penn family at this period, through their extravagancies, needy, a remarkable spirit of accommodation was extended to him, such as we believe was given to no other individual. He was a prudent business man and at once made use of his power in selecting and taking up only such lands as suited him. As for Indian rights or claims, he had as little regard for them as those he dealt with, providing he could have their strong arms to shield and protect him. Thus in 1727 and 1728, he purchased thousands of acres of the best land above the Kittatinny or Blue Mountains—one tract of five thousand acres in 1735 at the present Nazareth, and three thousand acres in 1736 in six parcels along the Lehigh river, in and around the present Allentown, which in consequence was called after him. These tracts, it must be remembered, were all purchased some time before the Walk and without any right or even the knowledge of the Indians. He had the sagacity in selling these lands to purchasers to omit the date when he received said grants. This, in our observations among records outside of his transactions, was an unusual proceeding, and there is no question but what there was an understanding on this subject with Thomas Penn. It is remarkable too with what success the secret was kept, especially of the lands around Dingman's Ferry, twenty-four miles above the Blue Mountains, regularly surveyed and purchased by him upwards of nine years before the Walk. The running of the line from the termination of the one and a half day's journey to near the mouth of the Lackawaxen on the Delaware, was done no doubt chiefly to accommodate him so as to be rid the sooner of Indian claims. In his visits to Durham Iron Works on and after 1727, he tells us, he there became acquainted with Tishcohan, Nutimus and Tedyuscung.

Mr. Allen was mayor of Philadelphia in 1735, and recorder from 1741 to 1750. He was commissioned chief justice of the Supreme Court, September 20, 1750, and continued in the office till the spring of 1774, when owing to the troubles of the times he resigned. It will thus be seen that he had much experience in public affairs. He was married to Margaret, the daughter of Andrew Hamilton, the celebrated lawyer, and the sister of Lieut. Gov. James Hamilton. He had sons, Andrew, William, John and James, who at first were vacillating, but in the end proved royalists. It is said, in 1761, he was only one of three persons in Philadelphia who kept a coach drawn by four horses and driven by an imported coachman. Much of his wealth as well as his positions he owed to the Penns, and with the troubles of the Revolution approaching, as a royalist, he was placed in no enviable situation. Accustomed to regard the King as the source of power, the proprietaries as only secondary, and the popular cause increasing, he concluded to leave his native land for an asylum in Great Britain, where he resided until his death in September, 1780. Unlike the Penns, Mr. Allen was a man of enterprise and public spirit. The college in Philadelphia was chiefly established through his and Dr. Franklin's exertions. The latter, while in command of a regiment, named Fort Allen, on the Lehigh, after him in 1756. Mr. Allen, from his strong prejudices and his devoted attachment to the interests of the Penns, was not qualified to sit as an impartial judge in the Supreme Court. An examination of his papers also indicates that he had not the ability requisite for that position.

Mr. Allen's correspondence reveals that he was importunate for office, as confirmed by the following extracts: Gov. John Penn, in a letter to his uncle Thomas, dated Philadelphia, March 17, 1764, thus expresses himself: "Before I finish I must observe that many good people in this city have been disgusted at the particular regard always paid that gentleman's recommendations to every office that fell vacant, in prejudice to any pretensions they might have from their own merit and superior qualifications, and look upon themselves as neglected and unnoticed only because they happen to be obnoxious to him. I take him to be a very good man, but too easily biased at the expense of his judgment, and very open to flattery, fond of popularity, but mistaking the ends of obtaining it." In reply to his nephew's letter respecting his contemplated marriage, Thomas Penn does not appear to give his hearty approval. Under date of London, April 12, 1765, he says: "In this case you must on considering it closely be of opinion that the party who think Mr. A. and his friends direct every thing, will suppose with great reason that his influence will be greatly increased, and on appointment of any one of his family to an office they will make great clamor and say all offices are to be swallowed up by them; his family is numerous, this must cause other connections, and it will be a very difficult part for a governor to refuse applications from persons he must necessarily be under great influence to oblige. Besides considering how ready the people are to suppose we have an undue influence over our judges, and even now press us to an appointment during good behavior, can it be thought they will not increase the clamor of their governor, the next heir to one of the Proprietors should marry the Chief Justice's daughter. I think Mr. A. could not prudently continue in the office, that we could not with any degree of prudence permit him, tho' I believe a man of too much honor to be under any influence."

The aforesaid John Penn was the son of Richard. He came over in 1763 as Lieutenant Governor of the Province, and was married to Ann, the daughter of Mr. Allen. In 1764 he offered increased bounties for the killing and scalping of all Indian enemies above ten years of age. He was very near-sighted, possessed the reserved family characteristic, and by no means popular. He died in Bensalem, Bucks county, in 1795, aged 67 years. He was buried in Christ Church yard and afterwards taken up and carried to England, "thus adding," as John F. Watson remarks, "to the strange aversion which members of the Penn family generally showed to remaining with us, either living or dead."

BENJAMIN EASTBURN.

As surveyor general of Pennsylvania at the particular request of Thomas Penn, Benjamin Eastburn was present at the Walk for the purpose of noting the distances and making a map of the same, assisted by his deputies, Nicholas Scull and John Chapman. Of his early history we know little more than that he was born in the year 1696 and resided a brief time in Abington township, where he married Ann Thomas 29th of 8-mo., 1722. He was appointed to succeed Jacob

Taylor as surveyor general Oct. 29, 1733, and continued in said office until on or near his death, his successor being William Parsons, who was commissioned August 22, 1741. We are satisfied that he was not present at the Trial Walk in 1735, it being in charge of John Chapman. At the termination of the one and a half day's journey he ran the line in a northeast direction to near the mouth of the Lackawaxen, a distance of about sixty-six miles, and requiring four days' additional labor.

That Mr. Eastburn did not perform an honorable part in this transaction is certain from his map, both in the manner he conducted the survey and endeavored to conceal thereby the advantages taken of the Indians, which however his employer may have imperatively demanded from a too complying agent. As surveyor general, by the direction of Thomas Penn, he laid off many thousand acres of land in the present county of Northampton, in the years 1735 and 1736, which had been sold to purchasers, and which he must have known had never been acquired by any right or purchase from the Indians. He says on his map, "A day and a half's walk on the 19th and 20th of September, 1737, by Edward Marshall and James Yates, being about sixty miles." This statement is very ingenious and worthy of Thomas Penn himself. The whole distance marked on the map was not walked by the two, James Yates having given out sometime before, but together they may have gone the sixty miles; and if they had it is still incorrect, for it should have been not less than sixty-six, and perhaps nearer seventy-two. Neither does he give the distance on the northeast line, but instead says "a right line through a mountainous, barren country"—the object being to get in all the Minisink territory above the Blue Mountains sold nine years before to William Allen, under a pretext of "a right line," and deceive by a "barren country," as if there was no good land within the purchase. The map thus leaves the impression that whatever was comprised within the Walk could possess little value. The next fact is, as to the starting point. He places the beginning of the Walk at the intersection of the Durham road and Newtown township line, and yet the mass of evidence states and is confirmed by tradition that the walkers actually started about a mile further up so as to be enabled to extend the journey that much more at its close. This was another cheat which he has knowingly through his presence striven to cover. By John Chapman's memoranda of the Trial Walk he found the distance from Wrightstown to the Lehigh river 39 miles. Applying Eastburn's scale to his map the distance is but 32 miles, which, to the present town of Bethlehem, where the river was crossed, is incorrect.

Respecting his defence before the King against the Delaware Indian complaints presented by Dr. Franklin, Thomas Penn thus writes under date of London, March 11, 1757, to his secretary, Richard Peters: "Of the Map of Benjamin Eastburn, on looking over which I observe what you say as to the head line going the shortest way to the River Delaware, instead of being run at right angles. I do not know that any line was run, or what was done upon it, that you will find by the Letters and Minutes at the time, but you know and will observe that we do not claim any above the Kittannin Mountains, which is almost as short a distance to the Delaware as any other by virtue of this Purchase; and as to the walk to that place, it cannot be above forty miles, as you say the whole is not more than fifty. I am very well pleased you have found some Minutes of my having blamed Benjamin Eastburn for having ran into the lands of the Six Nations, in extending the Walk beyond Kittannin Hills, which you will remember to mention to the Indians."

In the foregoing there is a general lack of veracity. That Benjamin Eastburn did actually run the said northeast line, and that he was duly paid therefor, his own accounts would have shown. As to his not claiming any land beyond the Kittatinny or Blue Mountains in 1757 by virtue of said map and Walk, places him in a still worse fix had his opponents known it, by his having sold thousands of acres there to William Allen and others, almost thirty years previously, and chiefly a secret to this day, and which to our personal knowledge the records of Bucks and Northampton counties conclusively prove. As to the Walk being only thirty miles to the mountains, he must have known by said map was a falsehood, for it makes it forty-nine. We question that even Peters said that the whole was but fifty, when it really was somewhere between sixty-five and seventy-two miles. If he had blamed Benjamin Eastburn for extending the Walk so far, why did he not relinquish the land and disclaim selling beyond the mountains? Who will attempt to prove that the Six Nations had any bona fide claims there? His friend William Allen, under oath in 1762, five years later, said that all that land belonged to Tishcohan, Nutimus, and their descendants, who were Delawares.

Mr. Eastburn, in the spring of 1739, commenced surveying the boundary line between Pennsylvania and Maryland, to the Kittatinny hills in Cumberland county, a distance of one hundred and thirteen miles westward from the present state of Delaware. He made a report (Archives, Vol. I., p. 614), on the subject, at Philadelphia, April 24, 1740, by which we learn that he was appointed to the undertaking December 5, 1738, as principal surveyor, and Lawrence Growdon and Richard Peters to be present as commissioners on the part of Pennsylvania. In a letter from Thomas Penn to Richard Peters, dated London, February 8, 1743, he reflects severely on his character: "We all look upon Benjamin Eastburn's secreting the Tract of Land so long before surveyed as a very dishonest action, and shall never allow his heirs to take one acre of it, so that they need not expect the least favor." Mr. Eastburn resided in 1733, in Lower Merion, where it is supposed he subsequently died.

NICHOLAS SCULL.

The subject of this sketch was the son of Nicholas and Abigail Scull, who settled in Whitemarsh, where it is known the family had resided for some time. He was born October 26, 1701, and must have received for this early day a fair education. That he was of studious habits is confirmed by Franklin in his autobiography, who says that he was a member of his club and that he "loved books and sometimes made verses." Having acquired a knowledge of the Indian language, he was occasionally employed by the government and others as interpreter. In May, 1728, he was sent by Governor Gordon with his brother, John Scull, to treat with the Indians about some difficulties that had occurred at Manatawny. In 1731 we know that he resided in Philadelphia, and for several years afterwards. As deputy of Benjamin Eastburn in the fall of 1736, he made several surveys in the vicinity of the present Bethlehem and Nazareth for those who had taken up tracts there. According to Samuel Preston, Edward Marshall about this time assisted him as a chain carrier. It is very likely owing to this circumstance that he became engaged in making the surveys at the time of the Walk in 1737. He also assisted in running the northeast line to the Delaware. Alexander Brown says in his testimony that on his return to Captain Harrison's at the upper Indian settlement, as well as at Hockyondocquay, the Indians expressed to Mr. Scull their displeasure at the way the Walk was performed.

Governor Thomas, in May, 1740, sent him to the Minisinks to settle a difficulty that had arisen between a white man by the name of Henry Webb and an Indian, by which the former was wounded. He was accompanied by John Lukens, and they had to hold their conversation, strange to say, with the Hollanders settled there, in the Indian language. They met with a very hospitable entertainment from the venerable Samuel Depue. In October, 1744, he was commissioned sheriff of Philadelphia county, which office he held for several years. In the previous August a delegation of the Six Nations, with Shickalamy and others, visited Philadelphia to arrange some matters of business, when he again performed the duties of interpreter, and also in July, 1745, for the Indians from Shamokin. Owing to ill health, William Parsons, the surveyor general, resigned his office, when Mr. Scull was appointed June 10, 1748, in his place. The county of Northampton was formed from Bucks in 1752, and the following year he was elected sheriff of the same, and continued in the office for three years, during which time he resided in Easton, after which he again removed to Philadelphia to follow surveying.

On the agitation of the complaints of the Delaware Indians against the conduct of Thomas Penn, Governor Denny through his orders acted for his defence, and on January 25, 1757, took Mr. Scull's deposition on the Walk. It may be seen in full in the Colonial Records

(Vol. VII., p. 399), and commences in a manner which is in itself sufficient evidence that as a witness he was neither disinterested nor impartial. "Mr. Nicholas Scull, surveyor general, came into Council, and acquainted the Governor that in September, 1737, he was present in running the Line of the Indian Purchase of the lands in the Forks of the Delaware, with respect to which the Proprietaries were, as he was informed, publickly charged with defrauding the Indians, that he had put down in writing what he remembered about it, and requested he might be examined thereto, which being done, he signed the Paper, and affirmed to Truth thereof before the Governor in Council and his affirmation was ordered to be entered as follows:" In his deposition, which was to be laid before the King, the foregoing was omitted, for the reason that it would appear that he was interested, and to have nothing said about the report of defrauding the Indians, while in the records here it should be entered as if he had voluntarily come forward to defend the proprietaries of so vile a charge. His principal testimony consists in stating that he believes the Walk was fairly performed, and that he had heard no Indians complain about it. He says the Walk was continued some distance beyond the Blue Mountains, and that the whole distance walked was about fifty-five statute miles. He is too much contradicted by several other witnesses that were also present for us to dwell on the veracity of his statements.

He could not have been ignorant as a surveyor of the true distance, and why did he not give that without any supposition? The favors he had received from the proprietaries in several ways and to which he was still beholden as surveyor general, were too strong for his better judgment, but there was perhaps a still stronger tie to bind him to Thomas Penn. He had prepared just then a large map of the Province, which he had dedicated to Thomas and Richard Penn, as "true and absolute Proprietaries and Governors," which the former was expected to liberally patronize. This map was published in 1759, and was entitled a map of the improved parts of Pennsylvania and Maryland, chiefly prepared from his own surveys. It was undoubtedly the first correct map published of the Province on a large scale, embracing more than half the present area of the State. Copies of it are rare, the writer having seen but one, and for that early time, when the population probably did not exceed 200,000, it exhibits certainly no small degree of enterprise.

Nicholas Scull was married to Rebecca Thompson October 7, 1732, and had children, Nicholas, John, Jasper, James, Mary, Abigail, Edward and Elizabeth. Nicholas, his eldest son, was married to a daughter of Solomon Jennings, and he has been mistaken by several writers for his father. The latter died in the fall of 1761, and was succeeded the following December by John Lukens, of Horsham. It will be seen by the foregoing that he held the office of surveyor general for thirteen years, besides a number of other official positions. As Indian interpreter, and for the publication of several valuable maps relating to the Province, he certainly deserves our regard. It is to be regretted that a man of his acquirements did not also devote a portion of his time to literature and the history of the times. This probably was prevented by his pecuniary condition, of which Richard Peters wrote in 1753, that though "industrious and enjoys a good office yet he has a large family and is not beforehand in the world." His five sons, it is said, were all surveyors. His grandson, William Scull, also published a large and complete map of the Province in 1770.

It may be mentioned that of the six depositions taken in behalf of Thomas Penn in 1757 relating to the Walk, Nicholas Scull's was the only one inserted in the minutes of the Council, for the reason of its being the most favorable; the five others were transmitted to England and probably no copies retained here. One thing is certain, that these depositions were kept concealed, and only such uses were made of them as was thought would best answer the purpose. Taken collectively they do not favor the proprietaries, and there is one evidence at least that they were tampered with after being first taken. Thomas Penn, in a letter to Richard Peters, dated London, May 12, 1757, appears not to have been fully satisfied with Mr. Scull's mention of the whole distance, and says: "I wish he had mentioned the distance to the foot of the mountains only."

TIMOTHY SMITH.

The parentage and early history of Timothy Smith we are unable to give, but as he lived for some time and died in the township of Upper Makefield, it may possibly be that he was a native of that section, for the surname is early known in that vicinity. He was first elected sheriff in 1728, and continued until 1730, and again from the fall of 1734 to 1737, when he was succeeded by John Hart. He was also county treasurer at various times. As it has been published that the Walk came off in the fall of 1733, it will be seen by this that he was not sheriff at that time. It was no doubt owing to his official position that led to his being appointed to have charge of the Trial Walk, and for which purpose he had been to the city with John Chapman and received his instructions personally from Thomas Penn. In April, 1735, it appears by the Penn Accounts that he selected, with John Chapman, the route, and had men employed to clear the way and mark the trees as a guide for the walkers to go by in the absence of roads and paths. The opening of the way involved considerable labor owing to its having been laid out by the compass to go in as direct a line as possible to the Lehigh Water Gap, if no further, leading part of the way through a very rocky, hilly country—as, for instance, through the present townships of Haycock, Springfield and Saucon. The total expense allowed him was £33, 7s, or $89.33 of our present currency.

Respecting the Walk of 1737, he says in his deposition that he "was employed by Thomas Penn, Esquire, one of the Proprietors of this Province, and James Steel, their Receiver General, to superintend the going a day and half's Walk." Edward Marshall, Moses Marshall and Joseph Smith, have respectively stated that Mr. Smith had offered a reward of five hundred acres of land to the one that should walk the farthest of the three in eighteen hours. We need not wonder that under such conditions, by the competition thus encouraged, there would be rapid walking, at the cost of the Indians and to the benefit of the proprietaries. Joseph Knowles, the nephew of Mr. Smith, and who was present and assisted at the Walk, says at about one o'clock of the first day "The Indians began to look sullen, and murmured that the men walked so fast; and several times that afternoon called out and said to them—you run—that's not fair—you was to walk. The men appointed to walk paid no regard to the Indians, but were urged by Timothy Smith and the rest of the proprietor's party." He was at this time in his forty-seventh year, and no doubt from the great age subsequently attained, must have been still in his prime. The sum allowed him for this service was £26, 2s, 2d, and which includes the expense of a change in the route, compensation and entertainment of the walkers and several assistants. In the fall of 1739 he was elected a county commissioner, and in 1752, with five others, had the building of Makefield Meeting House.

Owing to the repeated charges made against the conduct of the proprietaries toward the Indians and the investigation demanded, at the request of Thomas Penn Governor Denny summoned Timothy Smith to Philadelphia, before whom, March 15, 1757, he testified in regard to the Walk, only such evidence being set down, of course, as policy permitted. As far as it goes it appears to be pretty fair testimony, and admits the efforts made to have the Walk laid out as direct as possible, and that Benjamin Eastburn or Nicholas Scull had made use of a compass from the Indian settlement of Pocopoghcunk to the end of the Walk. That part of his evidence where he says the Proprietor did not covet so much land beyond the Blue Mountains was undoubtedly afterwards erased, as may be observed, with the view of this name not appearing, under any such circumstances, before the King. Hence we may conclude, where one such liberty was taken more followed, so as to garble and misconstrue as much as possible matters in favor of Thomas Penn, who, judging from his actions, was doubtless the guilty party.

As we learn by the Penn Accounts, Mr. Smith, John Heider and some other persons, were sent by the proprietary party to Easton in 1758 to attend the conference held there with the Indians and "to confront and confute the false stories raised about the Indian Walk," for which services they were allowed £20. He died in the beginning of May, 1776, at the advanced age of 86 years, leaving a wife Rachel and six children, namely: Timothy, Isaac, Joseph, Pleasant, Ruth and Rachel.

Owing his appointment and compensation to Thomas Penn, and to whose influence he was also indebted for his commissions as sheriff, it is no doubt these several matters biased him in his favor, at a time too when there was no opposing interests. He doubtless meant to do his duty to his employer, and it is very likely that he had no knowledge of the circumstances attending the Trial Walk and the Walk of 1737, *except as they revealed themselves*, and when too late found himself a party to proceedings from which, had he known in time, he would have shrank in amazement. However, he lived to see the consequences of a long Indian war and the powerful opposition engendered thereby, with the investigation of the matter, and, however innocent, it must have caused him serious reflections. As a witness he appears possessed of considerable candor with no undue partiality for the party that required his testimony. That he should, like John Chapman, have kept the Trial Walk so completely secret from his neighbors, or descendants, is remarkable, but he may have acted thus from an implied understanding with Thomas Penn, or from circumstances that it was not politic for him to reveal. Respecting his participation in the Walk, Richard Peters wrote from Philadelphia, November 22, 1756, to Thomas Penn: "Timothy Smith was then sheriff and had the direction of the whole affair, and is, I assure you, a man who will not favor the Proprietaries, nor disoblige the Quakers, who have extremely interested themselves in this inquiry."

JOHN CHAPMAN.

The subject of this sketch was the eldest son of John and Jane Chapman, born near Stanhah, Yorkshire, in 1679, who arrived here with his parents in 1684, and were among the earliest settlers of Wrightstown. He was early known as a practical surveyor there, having in 1719 divided the Park, as it was called, containing 650 acres in the centre of the township, among the adjoining landholders. In April, 1723, he laid out by order of the court the road leading from the county line near Governor Keith's residence in Horsham to the south corner of John Dyer's land, being at the present Cross Keys. This was in consequence long known in old deeds as Dyer's road, and now the principal highway passing through Doylestown towards Philadelphia.

At how early a period he was appointed deputy surveyor for Bucks county we are unable to state.

We do know that he was personally engaged by Thomas Penn to make the requisite surveys for the Trial Walk from Wrightstown to the Lehigh Gap if not further. For this purpose he was specially employed under the superintendence of Timothy Smith, then sheriff of the county. He commenced his labors April 22d, and did not get through till May 1, 1735, and by the Penn Accounts was allowed the sum of £4, paid him the following July 23d. This route passed up the Durham road to the present Gardenville, thence west of the Haycock and near the present villages of Strawntown and Appelbachsville. From his memoranda copied years afterwards by John Watson we learn that he made the total distance to the Kittatinny or Blue Mountains 48¾ miles. As related in a previous chapter the Trial Walk accordingly came off in the beginning of May, about which, as we learn from James Steel's correspondence, the proprietors were very anxious to know the result, particularly how far it had extended up into the country, so as to know the better how to treat with the Indians in relation to it at the next meeting held a few days afterwards at Pennsbury.

Thomas Penn appears to have been sufficiently satisfied with his services as to engage him for the one day and a half's walk of September, 1737, which employed him eight days in making the necessary surveys and in having the line of the Walk sufficiently cleared to expedite travel. The compensation given him for these services was £2, 8s. He was in his fifty-eighth year at the time of this occurrence, and must have certainly possessed a vigorous constitution for one of that age to have thus been enabled to undergo, as he did, all the fatigues of travel and exposure attending it. Near the close of 1739 he married Ruth Wilkinson, and died in 1743 at the age of 65 years. He left a son John who became a physician and the owner of considerable real estate in the county.

After the conclusion of John Chapman's labors respecting the Walk, it is reasonable to suppose that he could not have failed to observe therein the various studied and deep laid plans of Thomas Penn to take every possible advantage of the Indians. Having been a deputy surveyor of the county for twenty years and holding the office through the influence and consent of the proprietaries, may have been one reason why his participation therein remained so quiet and so completely escaped even the notice of the people of his neighborhood. From the Penn MSS. we also learn of his having been sent by James Logan in the fall of 1727 as a guide to the Minisinks in company with Nicholas Scull as Indian interpreter respecting the encroachments of the whites. In the chapter on Indian rights mention has been made of the displeasure exhibited by an Indian chief on his father having settled over the line of the Indian purchase, and of which it is most likely he must have had a knowledge. The evidence now is too strong to be rebutted that the walkers really started from a chestnut tree on the corner of his land a few rods above the meeting house, while Benjamin Eastburn on his map denoted its commencement about a mile below, which no doubt was the true line and agreed with the said Indian chief's observation. Now, as a life-long resident in the neighborhood and as an assistant in the survey, we cannot see how he could have been ignorant of a serious fraud practiced here in the very beginning of the Walk, and which has also so long remained a mystery and which he has done no more to reveal, explain or establish, than he has of the Trial Walk. Hence the question will arise, from his participation therein as a surveyor, how far can his reputation be creditably sustained.

JAMES YATES.

Like most of those mentioned in this work, the writer has heretofore seen no notice of this individual whatever, except an incidental allusion in connection with the Walk. His father, James Yates, arrived at Philadelphia as an indentured servant for five years with Henry Baker, in the Vine of Liverpool the 17th of 7-month, 1684. We know that he resided in Newtown township, Bucks county, some time before 1713, and that he sold this year a lot of land containing twenty-two acres for £16 to Daniel Doan, of the vicinity. He died in the spring of 1733, and by his will we ascertain that his wife Agnes survived him, and that he had the following children: Joseph, James, Peter, Robert, Sarah, Agnes, Margaret and Elizabeth. Judging by the foregoing, James may have been the second son, who we know was married to Rachel Routledge at Wrightstown in the fall of 1727.

There is no direct evidence that he was one of the three engaged in the Trial Walk of 1735, but the presumption is strong enough to warrant the belief, and that through this circumstance he was again employed to be one of the walkers in 1737. Thomas Furniss, in his statement, says: "At the time of the walk, I was a dweller at Newtown and a near neighbor of James Yates. My situation gave him an easy opportunity of acquainting me with the time of the setting out." It appears that on the first day of the Walk it was almost as much as Edward Marshall could do to keep up with him. On the forenoon of the next day, being rainy, Timothy Smith says from growing lame and tired he gave out just before they crossed the Lehigh river, which in the evidence was here called *Tobyhanna creek*, as is confirmed by N. Scull's map of 1759, probably about six miles before the journey was ended. John Heider, in his evidence, gives quite a different phase to the matter, for he says "that the said James Yates, having on the second day of the Walk drank rather too much, as he heard him declare, gave out and stopped, to the best of his remembrance about half an hour before the expiration of the time fixed, which was twelve o'clock at noon, but Marshall held out to the end of said time." In corroboration, Alexander Brown says that "a short time before the Walk was finished the said James Yates having drank rather too much gave out and stopped." There is no doubt at the time he gave out he must have accomplished at least sixty miles of the journey, to which Benjamin Eastburn on his map may probably have reference.

The next mention we find of him is in 1750, when by order of Abraham Chapman he was to receive from

the county treasurer for 17 squirrel scalps and one
wolf's head, the sum of £1, 4s, thus indicating that
he was, like the other walkers, fond of hunting at a period
when game was still abundant. Edward Marshall,
in his testimony, taken before Governor Denny,
March 1, 1757, states that "James Yates and Solomon
Jennings both since deceased." Again, in the report of
the Council on the Walk, January 6, 1758, mention is
made of Marshall as "survivor of the Walkers." This
would prove that he must have died somewhere between
1750 and 1757. In the Penn Accounts, mention
is made of £20 having been paid September
7, 1758, to "Heider, Yates and Smith for their attendance
at Easton to confront and confute the false stories
raised about the Indian Walk." Judging by this, the
Yates mentioned must have been some other person.
The family appear to have been in humble circumstances,
and we believe but few or none of the name
reside at present in the county. Samuel Preston was
therefore quite mistaken when he said he had been
informed "that James Yates, who led the way for thirty
miles or more, was quite blind when taken out of the
Durham creek and lived but three days afterwards."
This statement, in connection with the Walk, has been
repeatedly published, even quite recently.

SOLOMON JENNINGS.

The name of Jennings occurs as early as 1683 in Friends' Records of Burlington Monthly Meeting and is also mentioned in Philadelphia a few years later, hence the subject of this sketch may be either a relative or a descendant of one of those families. The earliest we know of him is that under a grant from the proprietors, dated March 5, 1736, he took up 200 acres of land in a bend on the south side of the Lehigh river about two miles above the present town of Bethlehem, on which he settled and chiefly resided the remainder of his days. It is our opinion that he was not engaged on the Trial Walk of 1735, but was afterwards substituted in the place of Joseph Doane. At a Council held at Philadelphia, Feb. 8, 1736-7, we learn "That one Solomon Jennings being recommended as a man of discretion and conduct, the sheriff had constituted him his deputy for the preservation of the peace and the execution of those warrants lodged with him for apprehending several of the rioters" at Wyoming on the west side of Susquehanna, and "to prevent any further violence from Higgenbothem and his associates."

From the services rendered he appears to have become somewhat of a favorite, for James Steel in a letter to Timothy Smith, dated August 27, 1737, in speaking of Edward Marshall, says, "when Solomon Jennings is expected to join and travel the day and a half with him." Whatever expectations had been formed of him as a walker were to be met with disappointment. On the first day of the Walk when he arrived about two miles beyond the Tohickon, at a place called Red Hill, which was between ten and eleven o'clock in the forenoon, he withdrew from the contest, and, as John Heider says, continued "with the rest of the company till they came to the west branch of Delaware; he there left them entirely and returned home." The distance traveled from Wrightstown to Red Hill was about eighteen miles.

From the Northampton county records we learn that on the formation of the county in 1752, his petition was granted to keep a public house, and in 1753 the court appointed him an overseer of highways in Salisbury township, where he resided, and which office he retained for several years. In October, 1755, he was elected one of the county commissioners. On the breaking out of the Indian War he was appointed to the command of a company, in the fall of 1756 passed through Nazareth and the Wind Gap to scour the woods in search of the enemy and the bodies of those that may have been slain beyond the mountains. It appears he did not long survive this service, hastened perhaps by exposure, for he died February 17, 1757, and was buried near his residence, where his grave may be seen. Edward Shippen, in December, 1755, speaks of him as a "courageous and resolute fellow."

His will, which we have examined, is written on parchment and quite lengthy. To his name is affixed his mark, possibly indicating that he could not write. He appears to have been possessed of some property. He appointed his sons John and Isaiah, and his son-in-law Nicholas Scull, his executors. His children's names mentioned therein are John, Rachel, Elizabeth, Isaiah, Susanna, Ezekiel and Judith. The death of Solomon Jennings occurred but twelve days before the examination of Edward Marshall, and had he lived but a little longer he would also have been required to give his testimony respecting the Walk in behalf of the proprietaries. John Jennings, his eldest son, became sheriff of Northampton in 1762, and again in 1768, and proved himself an energetic officer in the Wyoming troubles.

INDIANS.

Concerning the Indians that once inhabited this section of Pennsylvania there will always be felt considerable interest. Though without civilization, and but a very rude knowledge of the arts, they were yet a people endowed with some of the noblest traits. Perhaps the aborigines of no other country possessed so free a form of government, and to which talent alone was the only qualification for position and preferment. Many of the relics of barbarism found in Europe were unknown among them. They had neither castes nor rank, nor even hereditary privileges, which have been so long the bane of the old world, and the means of elevating the few at the expense of the many. Our Indians were endowed with too manly and independent a spirit to tolerate the degrading effects of inferior position. There were no feudal laws or privileges for the benefit of the few; all had an equal right to the lands, to the game and to the fruits of the earth, without any restriction or limitation whatever. This condition had doubtless prevailed among them for thousands of years. When the whites came here they were justly astonished at their covetousness for lands, on which they had set no particular value except so far as it benefited all. This will account why the Penns, who alone had the power to deal with them, found it so easy to take every advantage. The forcing of the Minisink lands from them, their favorite hunting grounds, in the manner they did must redound to their eternal disgrace, and for which they fought with so determined a resistance to recover as to cause Governor John Penn to order them to be most wantonly butchered and scalped. The Indians who were concerned in the Walk by which they were so grossly wronged deserve a tribute to their memory.

SASSOONAN.

The earliest we know of this chief was at a Council held at the house of Edward Farmer, in Whitemarsh, May 19, 1712, at which were present Governor Charles Gooken and several of his friends, besides a number of Indians. With Sassoonan, Ealochelan and Scholitchy were present, the latter being the principal orator. The next we know of him is in the deed of September 17, 1718, by which is purchased from him and six other Delaware chiefs for the proprietaries, all the land from Duck creek to the south side of the Lehigh Hills and from the Delaware river to the Susquehanna, being about one-eighth of the present area of the State. Even with this extensive purchase, made at this early period, the settlers kept encroaching beyond its boundary, which occasioned great anxiety and uneasiness among the Delawares; so much so that preparations had been made and alliances formed for war, which by prudence and skill was alone averted.

Logan, in a letter to James Steel, November 18, 1729, calls him "Sassoonan our very good friend." At a meeting in Philadelphia, August 13, 1731, the former said to him: "We will discourse to you about the lands you claim, and shall speak of those affairs." As to selling the lands, he replied he could not answer till he had discoursed with the rest of his people. Here we see the cause in part no doubt of James Logan writing unfavorably of him from Stenton, Oct. 18, 1736, to Conrad Weiser. In a joint letter to the proprietaries from Isaac Norris, Samuel Preston and James Logan, dated Philadelphia, Nov. 13, 1731, is this extract: "In 1718 a release was obtained of the chiefs of our Indians, for all the lands on this side of Lehigh Hills, and beyond these it was resolved no settlements should be made till the lands were purchased of the Natives. In the mean time all possible care was taken to preserve Sassoonan or Ollamapis, the old King of our Delaware Indians, and the two young men who were to succeed him in strict friendship with us till on your coming over, which they were constantly given to expect that a Treaty might be concluded." The said young men, it appears, were Opekasset and Shackalawlin, who died shortly after said chief, one from small-pox and the other from an accident. Attention is here called again to the repeated violation of the foregoing declaration that beyond said Hills " it was resolved no settlements should be made till the lands *were purchased from the natives.*"

The Penn Accounts tell us of several visits Sassoonan paid, with other Indians, to Philadelphia in January, 1732, August, 1733, and July, 1734, for which their expenses had been borne. On the very day of the Walk several barrels of meal are mentioned as having been sent to him costing £2. August 18, 1740, C. Grassold is allowed for making him a coat, &c., £3, 2s, 7d. As we see by the foregoing that he was still living, it must appear remarkable why he should have been entirely omitted with Shickalimy and Civility in the release of August 25, 1737. There is certainly cause here for suspicion of unfair dealing. On this matter Charles Thomson, in his *Alienation*, published in 1759, (p. 36) remarks: " It was therefore necessary in order that things might be carried on quietly, that the Deed of 1718 should be passed over in silence, and that Sassoonan should not be present or any of those who signed that deed."

At a meeting held in Philadelphia before Governor George Thomas, from July 6 to 12, 1742, we find Sassoonan or "Olumapies, chief of the Delawares of Shamokin," as he is styled in the proceedings; at the conclusion of which, with Nutimus, he was most grossly insulted in a speech made by Conassatego, an Iroquois chief, at the instigation of the Governor, who gave them immediate orders to remove from the territory they occupied and claimed or he would see that it should be done. In a letter from Conrad Weiser to Logan, dated Tulpehocken, September 27, 1747, he mentions that he had heard that Sassoonan or Olumapies was dead, but was not positive as to the fact.

SHICKALLMY.

However little known, this chief appears to have been of some note among the Indians, being mentioned in October, 1704, by James Le Tort. In a letter from James Logan to John Petty in 1728, he states: "Pray by all means bring Shakellamy either with you or as soon after as may be with conveniency. Tell him particularly that as he is set over the Shawaneh Indians, I hope he can give a good account of them; they came to us strangers, about thirty years ago; they desired leave of this government to settle amongst us as strangers, and the Conestogoe Indians became security for their good behavior. They are also under the protection of the Five Nations, who have set Shickellamy over them."

Respecting this chief of the Oneidas, Logan wrote to Thomas Penn, Nov. 13, 1731: "Shakellamy, one of the Six Nations, was despatched with a small but handsome present to invite some of their chiefs hither to treat of some affairs nearly concerning their own safety. That man has always been looked upon as sincerely our friend and entirely to be depended on. We just now hear he is returned to his own house about one hundred and twenty miles distant and those people will be with us in the spring as he says." The inference from these extracts is evident that he was instigated to lend his aid in keeping the Delawares and Shawanese in submission prior to their forcible removal from the Minisinks.

In the Penn Accounts we find eight bushels of wheat being delivered to him in 1733, and about the time of the Walk, meal to the value of £2, 7s, 8d. Again, Feb. 9, 1738, a hand vice and a saddle costing £2, 2s, 9d. He was present with a delegation of the Six Nations and several other Indians in Philadelphia at the meeting held in July, 1742, and August, 1744. On the latter occasion Nicholas Scull acted as interpreter. Conrad Weiser wrote, April 15, 1746, that "Shickelimy is to be depended on very much in Indian affairs." This is the latest information we have obtained respecting him.

TISHCOHAN.

From an affidavit made by William Allen in 1762, we learn that as one of the owners of Durham Iron Works, he became, whilst on his visits there, personally acquainted with "Tishecunk, who was reputed to be an honest upright man," and with "Nutimus had always been esteemed to be the chief original owners of the land in and about the Forks of Delaware and adjacent lands above Tohiccon." This, coming from the great land speculator, is pretty good evidence that they had recognized rights there, and that any dissent from either as regards unfair dealings in obtaining said lands must be of some weight. By his own oath, as we shall see, Allen has farther implicated himself with the Penns in depriving at least those Indians of a considerable portion of their lands, long before they had obtained any right to them, either by purchase or treaty, as has been mentioned in a previous chapter.

By appointment, Tishcohen and Nutimus, in October, 1734, had met John and Thomas Penn at Durham in relation to a treaty and sale of lands, and also in May, 1735, at Pennsbury, but no particular business was accomplished, except to have the Trial Walk secretly made in order to have things in readiness for the signing of the release for the Walking Purchase, which was duly concluded in Philadelphia in the presence of Thomas Penn, William Allen, James Logan and others, August 25, 1737, and to which Tishcohan,

Nutimus and two other Delaware chiefs affixed their marks, which was walked out so rapidly the following 19th and 20th of September by Edward Marshall that Solomon Jennings and James Yates were compelled to succumb. From the testimony of Ephraim Goodwin, who was present at the Walk, we learn that Tishcohan was then an aged man, and lived at the Indian village called Hockendocqua, near which the walkers and company staid over night on their first day's journey.

Like nearly all Indian names, it has been variously spelled or called, as Teshakomen, Tiscoquam and Captain John Tishekunk, perhaps according to the fancy of the several writers. The Historical Society have in their possession two original portraits, one of Tishcohan and the other of Lappawinzo, presented by Granville Penn in December, 1834. They cannot fail to be regarded with interest, for it is said of all the early Indians once inhabiting Pennsylvania those are the only ones existing, and by the Penn Accounts we learn were painted by order of John Penn in the summer of 1735 by Hesselius. In this portrait, which is nearly life size, he is represented with a Roman nose, a large mouth and several deep wrinkles reaching nearly across his forehead. He appears of a stout, muscular frame, about forty-five or fifty years of age, and what is singular for an Indian a bunch of hair is growing from his under lip and chin. He has a blue blanket around him, and a squirrel skin pouch hanging on his breast in which there is a plaster of Paris pipe, thus proving it to be his tobacco pouch and that he was a consumer of "the weed." His hair is so long as to be gathered together on the back of his head.

According to Heckewelder, Tishcohan means in the Delaware language "*He who never blackens himself.*" In referring to the likeness, we find the truth of this definition, in the absence of those daubs of paint with which many of the Indians were in the practice of disfiguring themselves. We are thus minute because few opportunities can occur of similar descriptions respecting those who so long dwelt here and occupied important if not conspicuous positions in our early history. We give the following extract from the report of the committee (Memoirs Historical Society, Vol. III., pp. 211-12,) respecting those portraits: "Of Lappawinzo we have been able to discover no further notice in history. James Logan speaks of him in 1741 as an honest old Indian. Tishcohan seems to have moved to the West, and was met by Frederick Post when he made his first journey to visit the Indians on the Ohio, in July, 1758. Such is the whole result of the inquiries of this committee, although they have examined all the documents printed and manuscripts within their reach. They have only to regret that they have been able to give so little interest to their Report, and that so little has been handed down to us of the history of the only two chiefs of the Lenni Lenape whose portraits have been preserved."

NUTIMUS.

The earliest we know of this chief is in the Penn Accounts, where mention is made that Joseph Hitchcock was paid Nov. 16, 1732, £1, 6s "for entertaining Nutimus and co." We next learn that in company with Tishcohan and Tunam he visited Thomas Penn June 9, 1733, on matters relating to lands. On the proprietaries' trip to Durham in October, 1734, it appears he resided at the Nockamixon flats, some six miles distant, to which a messenger had been sent for his presence. On this occasion he complained of the increasing encroachments of the whites and expressed a disposition to act a fair part with them. He was also at Pennsbury, May 9, 1735, being a few days after the Trial Walk, of which of course he was ignorant.

In a letter of instructions from James Logan to Conrad Weiser, Oct. 18, 1736, he speaks unfavorably of Nutimus; that he was a Jersey Indian and had no right to lands on this side the Delaware, and that he wanted to excite a war between the Indians and the English. He is also unfavorable therein to Sassoonan and Manawhyhickon, the latter being one of those who signed the deed of Aug. 25, 1737, for the Walk. We cannot learn that Nutimus was present at the Walk, or that he even had any knowledge of its coming off, yet according to Allen's testimony in 1762, he was one of the original owners of the lands above Tohickon and the Forks. On ascertaining the results of the Walk, he became still further dissatisfied and in consequence his name is found attached, with those of six other Indians, to the paper sent to Judge Langhorne, dated Smithfield, Jan. 3, 1740–41, in which they complain of the continued encroachments of the whites, and that it *was not safe for the lives of any persons to take their part.* As a result, when Nutimus, Sassoonan and the other Delawares went to Philadelphia in July, 1742, to attend a Council with Governor Thomas, the latter instigated Conassatego, an Iroquois chief, through presents given him, to grossly insult them, and order them at once to remove from the lands they occupied or else he would enforce the demand.

Of the foregoing, Gordon, in his History of Pennsylvania (pp. 253–4), makes the following remarks: "During the administration of Governor Thomas in 1742, the Indians complained that the walkers who outstripped them, ran, and did not pursue the course of the river, as they anticipated. The chief Nutimus, and others, who signed the treaty of 1737, refused to yield peaceable possession of these lands, and declared their intention to maintain themselves by force of arms. Under these circumstances, the proprietaries invoked the interposition of the Six Nations, whose authority over the Delawares was well known. Upon this invitation, a deputation of two hundred and thirty from those powerful tribes visited Philadelphia, where they were met by delegates from the Delawares, who had also been invited." On which occasion they were ordered to leave their lands, though reserved in the deed of 1737, in the presence of Thomas Penn, the right to "be permitted to remain on their present settlements and plantations, though within that purchase, without being molested."

Samuel Preston, in a communication written in 1826, says that Nutimus and his daughter lived in a cabin for some time in Nockamixon, and had been regarded as a physician, and that he was then "a feeble gray headed old Indian who could not speak much English." Col. Shippen, in a letter dated Fort Augusta, Jan. 20, 1758, states that several "small parties of Delaware Indians have arrived here with skins to trade at the store; among them old King Nutimus." The Rev. David Zeisberger gives him an excellent character; that he was born near Philadelphia, and never drank liquor; that his name implies *a striker of fish with a spear*, and that he moved with his brother Isaac to Ohio, a short time before 1750, where he died on the Muskingum in 1780.

LAPPOWINZO.

At the treaty held at Pennsbury May 9, 1735, with John and Thomas Penn, the proprietaries, this chief distinguished himself as the principal orator. On this occasion Nutimus, Tishcohan, Lesbeconk and others were present. Another meeting was agreed upon in Philadelphia, which was accordingly held on the 24th and 25th of August, 1737, in the presence of Thomas Penn, and on the latter day Lappowinzo, Manawhyhickon, Tishcohan and Nutimus signed the release for the Walking Purchase, witnessed by fourteen whites and twelve Indians. Barefoot Brinston acted as interpreter.

From the Penn Accounts we receive sufficient information to believe that the portraits of Lappowinzo and Tishcohan were taken by order of John Penn during the Pennsbury meeting by Hesselius, a Swedish artist. Lappowinzo is represented as a stout Indian of about forty years of age. A few black marks are painted on his forehead and cheeks. His hair is long and brought to the back part of his head, with a blue blanket thrown around him and a pouch on his breast fastened to his neck.

From Edward Marshall's testimony, taken in 1757, we learn that on the night of the first day's Walk they lodged near an Indian town called Hockyondocquay, and that early next morning Nicholas Scull, Benjamin Eastburn and another person went to said settlement and spoke with Lappowinzo, who lived there, to send some other Indians to accompany the walkers for the remaining distance, when he replied "that they had got all the best of the land and they might go to the Devil for the bad and that he would send no Indians with them." He further stated that about eight weeks after the Walk he was again at the Indian town, when the same chief said that "they were dissatisfied with the Walk, and that they would go down to Philadelphia the next May with every one a buckskin to repay the proprietor for what they had received from him and take their land again." He also complained that the

Walk was not fairly performed, and should not go the course fixed on by the proprietors, but should have gone along the Delaware, or by the nearest Indian path, as the proper direction. Alexander Brown, in his evidence, corroborates the foregoing.

It was Lappowinzo that Moses Marshall had reference to in his reminiscences taken down by John Watson, Jr., in a visit in 1822, in which "An old Indian said 'no set down to smoke, no shoot a squirrel, but lun, lun, lun all day long.'" By this it would appear he had been pretty well up in years. Heckewelder says that his name signifies *going away to gather food*. It would seem by some of the statements as if he had been chiefly instrumental in the selection of John Combush, Neepaheilomon alias Joe Tuneam, who could speak English, and his brother-in-law, Tom, the three young men appointed on the side of the Indians to be present as deputies to see that the Walk was fairly performed. James Le Tort, an Indian trader, mentions dealings with Lappowinzo in 1704, if not somewhat earlier. According to the report of the committee on his portrait, James Logan, in 1741, mentions him "as an honest old Indian."

LIFE OF EDWARD MARSHALL.

CHAPTER I.

HIS EARLY CAREER.

An interest taken in the life of an individual usually extends itself to his family and to the name by which it is known and distinguished from others. By its very signification the name of Marshall could not likely have originated from humble circumstances or applied to a lowly condition of life. It has about the same application in English as in French and German; in its general sense an office, particularly given in ancient times to one who had command of all persons below the dignity of princes. As a surname it is in consequence known from an early period, as is confirmed by works treating on heraldry. At the present time it has a broader application, and its orthography varies to conform to the language that uses it. Judging by Burke's General Armory, there are now a number of families bearing it in Great Britain.

As to the ancestry of Edward Marshall the opinions of his descendants vary, some stating that he was born in England; but this we do know that he was here at least when quite a young man and prior to 1733. In his examination before Governor Denny in 1757, he said that he was "of the people called Quakers," aged forty-two years and "a husbandman" by occupation. According to the inscription placed on his tombstone by his family he was born in 1710, but on the authority aforesaid in 1715. One tradition is that he was twenty-four years old when he performed the Walk, which would make it about 1713. The greatest discrepancy here is, however, but five years, and the latter date would prove a medium. One century and three-quarters ago is no inconsiderable lapse of time, which records alone can make clear. These facts are mentioned as some of the many instances of the difficulties that beset historians and biographers at the very commencement of their labors.

Samuel Preston, in a communication written in 1826, says Marshall was a native of Bucks county, but this is questionable. There is a family tradition that he was either born or lived when quite young in or near Bustleton, Philadelphia county, that he subsequently resided in the vicinity of Newtown, for a long period the county seat of Bucks; was passionately fond of hunting, and to his having served several surveyors as chain carrier, especially Nicholas Scull and perhaps Benjamin Eastburn. It may be that it was through this acquaintance and from a residence in the vicinity that led to his being selected one of the three to attempt what has since become so widely and popularly known as the Indian Walk, which was afterwards to be reported and laid before the King. He had at least three brothers, William, Moses and John, and a sister Rebecca. The former two it would appear were older than himself. From this it would seem probable that the father may have accompanied the family here if he did not actually precede it.

Edward was married, it is believed, in 1735 or the following year. According to his descendants his first wife was Elizabeth Oberfeldt, anglicized Overfelt or Overfield. She was of German origin and a resident of New Jersey. No doubt the acquaintance was in part brought about by a brother a short time previously having married his sister. Edward, with his brothers William and Moses, made application for unsettled lands above Tohickon creek, and for which warrants were granted as early as 1733. In consequence, Nicholas Scull, deputy surveyor general, laid off the lands on the 9th of May, 1738, in three tracts. Edward's contained 164 acres and 114 perches, the east corner of which touched on the Delaware, stated to be bounded on the east by the London Company's land and on the south by Mathew Hughes'. William Marshall's 162 acres and 117 perches were laid off adjoining his brother's tract on the northwest. Moses Marshall's tract of 174 acres and 28 perches was laid off about three-fourths of a mile west of the above, and we infer from the original draft is the tract that contains the present Marshall's graveyard, which will account for its location from near this early period.

These several tracts were taken from what was known as the Streiper Tract, containing originally four thousand four hundred and forty-eight acres, and purchased of William Penn in March, 1682, by John Streiper, a native and resident of the Duchy of Juliers on the borders of Germany. It was actually located, surveyed and laid off to him the 26th of March, 1703, and confirmed under the great seal of the Province the 24th of June, 1705. Now the said John Streiper, also his attorney, and after his death in 1717, his heirs, state in a petition that they had tried in various ways to sell, but in vain, alleging that all their endeavors on this matter "had no effect, because of a claim made to the land by the Indians, who say they never yet sold it." This matter, sorely against their wishes and earnest remonstrances, lingered until 1725, when it was, through the hands of James Logan, returned to the heirs of Wm. Penn. We have in this a strong instance of a powerful virtuous sentiment prevailing among the mass of the people here, not only in respect to their own rights but those of others. This curious bit of history has only recently come to light through the original documents obtained in England. But this is only one of numerous other exceptions of which no records have been yet produced, that the Indian title thereof had been previously extinguished even at so long a period before the Walk, thus actually confirming what the Indians have always claimed, that north of the Tohickon the lands had been sold by the Penns and settled upon by the whites without any previous compensation to or purchase from them. It was no doubt owing to this circumstance that immediately after the Walk the Marshalls were induced to locate and settle on their respective tracts, as well as the other early immigrants to this section, for we possess no knowledge of any having preceded them.

The names of these three brothers in corroboration is found with twenty-three others on a petition to the Court of Quarter Sessions of Bucks county, dated March 12, 1738, asking for the organization of a new township to be called "Tennicunk," in which they call themselves "divers inhabitants of the lands adjacent to Plumstead." Thus soon after came the present township of Tinicum into existence, so long the homes of the Marshalls, and where now reside hundreds of their respected descendants and still holding many acres of its best soil. It was through this family that it derived its name. The tract of William Marshall lay immediately opposite what has been so long known as Marshall's Island, but not approaching the Delaware by about half a mile, a strip of the London Company's land intervening. Having become its earliest possessor, he called it Tenicunk, being its original Indian name, which in the Delaware language signified an island covered with timber, and Tekene or Tacony, a place abounding with woods.

The first public road to this section was laid out by John Watson the 7th, 8th and 9th of June, 1747, from the landing at London Ferry (now Frenchtown) by the mouth of Tinicum creek, crossing the Tohickon at

Mearn's Ford and striking the Durham road at where is now Hinkletown, being twelve miles and thirty-one perches in length, the name of said ferry being derived from the London Company's purchase, which lay here immediately along the river and extending northwards from Edward Marshall's corner. The opening of this highway no doubt greatly promoted the improvement of this section. It was over the Durham road that the Walk was made, and which in 1746 was opened northwards to the iron works that gave it the name.

CHAPTER II.

HIS ACCOUNT OF THE WALK.

We have now approached, in these scanty materials regarding Edward Marshall, to the period of the "famous Walk," that through its results became so long a subject of intense interest not only throughout this country but in Europe, and upon which volumes were written during the sway of the Penns, who, it will appear, did not without cause style themselves "true and absolute Proprietors" of what is now the noble Commonwealth of Pennsylvania. The Penn Papers, acquired a few years ago in England, reveal the singular fact that before a meeting should take place with the Indians at Pennsbury, John and Thomas Penn had ordered a trial or experimental walk to be secretly made. For this purpose a road was opened through the woods and a survey made under direction of Timothy Smith, sheriff of Bucks county, James Steel, receiver general, and John Chapman, deputy county surveyor, all holding their commissions from the proprietaries. Steel sent a second letter, dated April 29, 1735, to the above named on this matter, in which he says: "The Proprietaries are very much concerned that so much time hath been lost before you began the work recommended so earnestly to you at your leaving Philadelphia; they now desire that upon the return of Joseph Doane, he together with two other persons who can travel well, should be immediately sent on foot on the day and half journey, and two others on horseback to carry necessary provisions for them and to assist in their return home. The time is so far spent that not one moment is to be lost; and as soon as they have travelled the day and half journey, the Proprietaries desire that a messenger may be sent to give them an account of without delay how far that day and a half travelling will reach up the country."

Two days after the signing of the release for the Walking Purchase of August 25, 1737, James Steel wrote to Timothy Smith that "the time for walking over the land is to be the 12th of September next, and for that purpose our Proprietor would request thee to speak to that man of the three which travelled and held out the best when they walked over the land before to attend to that service at the time mentioned, when Solomon Jennings is expected to join and travel the day and a half with him. Thou art also requested to accompany them, and to provide such provisions for these men as may be needful on the occasion desired. John Chapman is also to go along and with you,—and be sure to choose the best ground and shortest way that can be found. The Indians intend that two or three of their young men shall be present and see the land fairly walked over." That man of the three who had "held out best when they walked over the land before," we have every reason to believe, was Edward Marshall, whom Thomas Penn was now again anxious to secure, the more successfully to accomplish his object, in the greatest possible extent of the walk. In consequence of the court being in session at Newtown, it was deferred until the following Monday (September 19th), when the Walk was commenced and completed the next day, the walkers accomplishing upwards of seventy miles in eighteen hours, averaging about four miles an hour. The several witnesses agree that the distance was traveled from Wrightstown to Durham creek in six hours, which may be fairly estimated at thirty miles, averaging five miles per hour, which may well be regarded as most extraordinary walking. Had this speed been maintained throughout, the distance made would have been ninety miles.

The narration of Edward Marshall, we believe, has not heretofore been published, and we shall therefore now present it as copied from the original document. We regret to say that owing to certain parts of it having become either purposely defaced, or obliterated through time, we are obliged to make a slight abridgment, which we suppose does not exceed one-sixteenth part of the whole. We have no doubt that, particularly near its beginning, some important information has thus become lost.

"The examination of Edward Marshall of Mount Bethel township, Northampton county, husbandman, aged forty-two years, taken the First day of March, 1757, who being of the people called Quakers on his solemn affirmation, accordingly saith: that on the

Twelfth day of September in the year 1737, as this affirmant believes, he was employed by Timothy Smith pursuant to a purchase and begun the said walk at six o'clock in the morning from a Chestnut tree in the line of John Chapman in Wrightstown, Bucks county: that they kept the great Durham road from Wrightstown which they were directed to go, about north northwest and continued walking by the said great road to Gallows Hill, and from thence by a lesser road till twelve o'clock noon and then halted at the Widow Wilson's plantation on a branch of Scook's creek in order to dine and stayed there fifteen minutes, and then set off again, continuing about the same course by an old beaten Indian path, and crossing Saucon and the Lehigh, where Bethlehem now stands; continued the walk by the same old Indian path till fifteen minutes past six o'clock in the evening, when they halted near an Indian town called Hockyondocqua and there stayed all night: saith that the reason of their continuing their walk fifteen minutes after six o'clock was to make up the time which had been taken up in their halting at noon as aforesaid. The next morning some of the company's horses having strayed away, they went about two hours in looking for them, and then returned to the station where they had fixt and left the staves in the evening before. They began the walk again without any Indians with them at eight o'clock from where they left off and continued it by the said old Indian path for about one hour, until they came to Pokopogheunck; then continued their walk through the woods north northwest by a compass, which this affirmant then carried in his hand, but had not used before; and pursuing that course all the time and the said Yates having given out and stayed at Tobyhanna creek, this affirmant continued the walk in company with Alexander Brown, who carried the watch, and Enoch Pearson, being both on horses, until two o'clock in the afternoon and then stopped, in order to close and determine said walk on the north side of Pokono Mountain, where they marked five Chestnut oaks by putting stones in the forks of them. This affirmant saith that the reason of his continuing to walk two hours after twelve o'clock noon was to make up for the same time which they had lost in the morning in seeking the strayed horses as aforesaid. That the said affirmant did not run all of said time of going said eighteen hours walk from beginning to the end thereof. This affirmant being asked why the Indians who were with them the first day did not continue the second half day, replied that the Indians who had set out with them in the morning of the first day left them the next morning. Nicholas Scull, Benjamin Eastburn, and another person whose name he has forgotten, went early the next morning to the Indian town half a mile distant, where the Delaware chief Lappawinso then lived, to desire he would send some other Indians to accompany the walkers for the rest of the walk, but they returned with the following answer from the said chief, which was that the said walkers had got all the best of the land and that they might go to the Devil for the bad, and that he would send no Indians with them. Being further asked if he had ever heard any of the Indians express any uneasiness about the said walk, saith that about eight weeks after performing said walk he happened to be in company with Lappawinso at the said Indian town of Hockyondocqua with Tishacunch and some other Indians, being the first time he had seen them after said walk, he then heard the said Lappawinso say that they were dissatisfied with the said walk and that they would go down to Philadelphia next May with every one a buckskin to repay the Proprietor for what they had received from him and take their land again, and complained that the said walk was not fairly performed nor the courses run as they should have been. That he has heard said Lappawinso and other Delaware Indians frequently say that the said walk should not go the course agreed on between them, the Indians and the Proprietors, for that they should have gone along the courses of the Delaware. This affirmant further saith, that the place where the said walk ended at the said Five Chestnut Oaks as aforesaid was as he believes twenty miles* or thereabouts beyond or to the northward of the Kittatinny Hills.

Subscribed and affirmed to by Edward Marshall, 2d March, 1757, before William Denny."

We must remember that the foregoing was taken upwards of nineteen years after the Walk, and the

---

*This distance, with John Chapman's survey to said mountains, would make the Walk sixty-nine and three fourth miles.

time set for its performance was to have been September 12th, but it was postponed until the 19th, which will account for the discrepancy in regard to the exact date. This testimony was brought about through the charge of Tedyuscung that the Proprietaries of Pennsylvania had defrauded the Indians of great quantities of lands, partly through this Walk and a forged deed. Governor Denny, before whom this testimony was taken, owed his position at that very time to the Penns and he cannot therefore be judged as impartial. We more particularly mean in omitting what did not suit his or their views, through the instructions that he may have previously received.

CHAPTER III.

REMOVES TO NORTHAMPTON COUNTY.

From his testimony on the Walk we learn that Edward Marshall, about the middle of November, 1737, had been at the Indian town of Hockyondocqua and at the time had a conversation with the Delaware chiefs, Lappawinzo and Tiscohan, who it appears resided there. Judging by the time of year he was no doubt on one of his usual hunting campaigns into that section, the location of which was but a few miles below the Lehigh Gap. At what time he removed his family from Tinicum to Mount Bethel township we are unable to state, but it was at least as early as 1752, judging from a record of wolf and fox scalps that he had then been paid for in Northampton county. His love for game and the pursuit of lumbering may also have materially aided in his coming hither. Further, his brother John Marshall and his nephews Abner and Benjamin Overfield, the sons of his sister Rebecca, also resided in this section but on the north side of the Mountain in Lower Smithfield township, as also several of his wife's relations, which may have given additional inducement. Jacobus or Cobus creek empties into the Delaware about four miles below the Mountain or Water Gap. It is our opinion that he resided within a mile or two of the mouth of this stream. One account makes it about eighteen miles from Easton, which would make it further south. However, this we know from his own statement that it was in Mount Bethel township.

It may be well enough before we proceed further to give at this period some account of Northampton county, which had been formed from Bucks in the spring of 1752. Easton had been laid out a town as early as 1738, but made very slow progress as regards growth until it became the county seat. At its formation Northampton is supposed to have contained between five and six thousand inhabitants, settled in ten townships, of which number about one-tenth were Scotch-Irish, three hundred Dutch in Smithfield, and the rest chiefly Germans. By the original Forks was meant all that section of country lying between the confluence of the Lehigh and Delaware rivers, extending northwards to the Kittatinny or Blue Mountain, or sometimes applied beyond this in the early settled portions. It contained ten grist mills at this time. According to N. Scull's map of 1759, Northampton county possessed several public roads; one extending from Easton through the Wind Gap thence northeast to Fort Hamilton, now Stroudsburg, by Broadhead's, thence to Depue's on the Delaware about four miles, thence up the same to Hyndshaw's eight miles, where was a mill, and also one at Quick's, sixteen miles further. A road is represented from Easton to Bethlehem and from thence to Philadelphia and one to Berks county.

As it has been published that Marshall's creek had received its name from Edward Marshall, we will here state that we cannot find that he had any residence in that vicinity and we believe that it was so called after his brother John Marshall who we know by records was still living there in 1774, having two children under twenty-one years of age residing with him and taxable for two head of cattle. This stream is about eight miles in length and is a branch of the Anolomink or Broadhead's creek, emptying into it about a mile from the Delaware. It is represented on N. Scull's map of 1759 and William Scull's of 1770, but we cannot find it named earlier than on Reading Howell's large map of 1792, without any mills being denoted along its course. It is a wild romantic stream and its scenery has formed favorite subjects for the painter.

As orders had been given by the British government that the conduct of the Proprietaries of Pennsylvania should be enquired into regarding their transactions with the Indians and the cause of the war, the Penns, in self-defence, secured the influence of their Deputy Governor, William Denny, who issued a summons on Edward Marshall, and by an express, January 23, 1757, conveyed him from his home here to Philadelphia and actually kept him there until the following March 2d before he was released for an account of his knowledge respecting the famous Walk, which has just been given. The charge made to the

Penns for his delivery in the city was £1, 18s, 6d, and he was rewarded with only £5 ($13.33) for about forty days' detention Of this affair Moses Marshall related to John Watson in 1820, that "a person came to their house with a summons for his father to appear before Lord Loudoun in Philadelphia, and was very particularly examined respecting the Walk, his account taken down in writing to be sent to England. While in Philadelphia he was strictly guarded by two grenadiers, and not suffered to talk to any other person respecting the Walk or his present business." After some research we are inclined to believe the foregoing an actual fact. Lord Loudoun's army was quartered in Philadelphia in December, 1756, and remained there until into the following spring, whilst he chiefly resided in New York. He proved to be an overbearing scion of the British aristocracy, dictating to both the Governor and Assembly through his instructions. In the Colonial Records (Vol. VII, p. 379) under date of March 21, 1757, we find that he had actually requested Governor Denny to issue warrants for the arrest of suspicious persons for confinement in the Philadelphia prison and he may therefore have been present at this examination. We know he was in the city a few days thereafter.

The following circumstance goes to show the silliness of some people. David Broadhead and Edward Biddle certified at Easton, July 27, 1757, (see Penna. Archieves, Vol. I, p. 244) that they had "heard William Marshall say the following words, or words to the same effect, namely, that the Proprietors had wronged the Indians out of their lands ; and he would prove it, and in that respect he abided with the Indians." This charge was made against the second son of Edward Marshall, who we know at this time was not over nineteen years of age, and after his mother had been killed by the Indians only about nine weeks. This Edward Biddle was the son-in-law of Nicholas Scull.

We have supposed that Rebecca Marshall was the wife of Paul Overfield, who we know was a taxable in Lower Smithfield in 1761 to 1765. Mention is made in the will of her brother William Marshall, deceased, in Tinicum, in 1757, of a legacy left to his two nephews Abner and Benjamin Overfield. The former in 1774 is stated to have two children under twenty-one and taxed for 130 acres of land with ten acres of grain, two horses, three cattle and ten sheep. The latter with one child under age, 80 acres of land, seven acres of grain, two horses, two cattle and seven sheep. The latter is mentioned in the census of 1790, as having in family eight persons, three being males. Paul Overfield, a smith, and probably a relative of the aforesaid, is also mentioned in 1774, as having eight children under twenty-one, 160 acres of land, seven in with grain, two horses, two cattle and seven sheep. In the census of 1790 we find also a William Overfield with a family of five, whereof three are females. Previous to 1775 these are all represented as living in Lower Smithfield, and in 1790 in Chestnut

Hill township, from which it had been formed. Sarah, the widow of Martin Overfield, was still living near Dingman's Ferry in 1845, aged ninety-one years, and was born in that section. William Overfield, her son, represented Monroe county in the Assembly fifty years ago. Conrad Overfield, of Monmouth county, served in the army during the Revolution. They appear to have been a numerous and respectable family in the Minisink region, and we cannot find, excepting Edward Marshall's wife, that any members thereof had been injured by the Indians.

CHAPTER IV.

INDIAN ATTACKS ON HIS FAMILY.

Indian hostilities began in this section November 24, 1755, by an attack on Gnadenhutten, a Moravian settlement situated on the east side of the Lehigh about twenty-eight miles northwest from Bethlehem, where eleven persons were killed. So vigorously did they prosecute the war in Northampton county that by September, 1757, from a list made out by Capt. Jacob Orndt, one hundred and fourteen persons were killed and fifty-two taken prisoners, of whom seven afterwards returned. Among these sufferers in December, 1755, was the Weiser family, and that of Edward Marshall in May, 1757, and in the following August. According to John Hackett's list, made down to December 19, 1755, upwards of fifty persons had been killed and forty-one houses burnt in the county among a sparse and widely scattered population within so short a time as four weeks.

A letter from Easton, dated 25th of December, 1755, states that "the country all above this town for fifty miles is mostly evacuated and ruined, excepting only the neighborhood of Dupue's five families which stand their ground. The people have chiefly fled into Jersey. Many of them have threshed out their corn, and carried it off with their cattle and best household goods, but a vast deal is left to the enemy; many offered half their corn, horses, cows, goods, &c., to save the rest, but could not obtain assistance enough to remove them in time. The enemy made but few prisoners, murdering almost all that fell in their hands, of all ages and both sexes. All business is at an end, and the few remaining starving inhabitants in this town are quite dejected and dispirited. Captains Ashton and Trump march up to Dupue's this day, and are to build two block houses for defence of the country between that settlement and Gnadenhutten, which when finished, the inhabitants that are fled say that they will return."

Another writer, under date of December 31, says that "Indians known to be principally from Susquehanna have during this month been making incursions into the county of Northampton, where they have already burnt fifty houses, murdered above one hundred persons and are still continuing their ravages, murders and devastations, and have actually overrun and laid waste a great part of the country even as far as within twenty miles of Easton its chief town, and for the more easy annoyance of our inhabitants and the better security of their prisoners and plunder these Indians have fixed their headquarters at Neskopeck, which is not thirty miles from the inhabitants."

From Franklin's paper, the *Pennsylvania Gazette*, of January 8, 1756, we learn that "The Quakers of this city have made considerable contributions for the relief of our frontier inhabitants, who have been lately driven from their settlements, and plundered of everything, by the savage cruelty of the Indians. And we hear from Bucks county, that some of the society there are collecting a quantity of corn, and other necessaries, for the like purpose. The calamitous circumstances of these unhappy people are much aggravated by the most horrid murders being committed on their nearest and dearest relations and friends, and by the present inclemency of the season. Wherefore it is to be hoped the example will become general, and that every one will assist according to his ability, in alleviating the distresses of his fellow subjects."

This state of affairs actually continued with but little intermission until into 1764, a period of over eight years, during which time scenes of the most atrocious character were enacted, as if each side endeavored to excel the other in cruelty, it appearing on the part of the Delaware and Shawanese Indians as their last and most determined efforts to secure the lands out of which they believed they had been unjustly defrauded by the proprietaries, and which records establish were conveyed unto William Allen as early as November 16, 1727, and from which afterwards forcibly dispossessed through a connivance with the powerful Iroquois.

After the Indian hostilities had fairly commenced, some time in the latter part of 1755, or in the following year, as a matter of security Edward Marshall removed his family into New Jersey where they remained until the spring of 1757, when apprehending the greatest danger over he returned to his former residence below Jacobus creek. Somewhere about the 23d or 25th of May in company with Matthew Hughes, a former neighbor of his in Tinicum, but now boarding with him, he went up the above named stream within three miles of the mountain to cut logs and while thus engaged a company of sixteen Indians attacked the house. One of them threw his match coat on a bee hive by the side of the garden, which caused the bees to rush out to sting them, which fortunately by arresting their attention enabled five of the youngest children to get off and conceal themselves among the bushes. The eldest daughter Catharine, aged about fourteen, was shot at in running; the ball entered her right shoulder and came out below her left breast, but she ran on and hid herself in a stream of water by which she staunched the flow of blood and eluded their search. They took no property but a coat belonging to Matthew Hughes, in the pocket of which was £3 in money. Mrs. Marshall they made a prisoner and at once proceeded northwards. Being within a month of becoming a mother and not able to travel fast enough, when they reached the mountain they killed and then scalped her.

From Captain Van Etten's Journal of the following 23d of June, we learn that a party of thirteen men from Jersey were making a search for the remains of Mrs. Marshall which had not yet been found. Some accounts say that they were not discovered for above six months afterwards. It is a family tradition that when found word was sent to the husband to visit them for identification. He readily satisfied himself by a peculiarly formed tooth and the dress she wore which was but little decayed. On examination the scull and breast bore evidences of the tomahawk and the remains of twins were discovered. Judge of the feelings of any man when placed under such circumstances. Edward Marshall had nine children living with this wife, of which several of the oldest may have been with him from home when the attack was made. Their names were Peter, William, Moses, Martin, Catharine, Elizabeth, Jemima, Naomi and Amy. The papers of the Friendly Association state that the Indians in going and returning on this expedition did no other mischief within eight miles of his house.

The second attack was made in August of the same year, by which his eldest son Peter Marshall was killed, but accounts of which greatly vary. One tradition is that he was shot whilst engaged in covering a stack. Another, that with others he had sought the protection of a fort, and without their knowledge the Indians had thrown down a fence and driven the cattle into a field of corn, which on being observed five young men rushed forth to them to turn them out and in so doing were fired at in ambush, killing two of the number, one being Peter Marshall. We are inclined to believe the first account the most probable. The date we are only enabled to fix from written evidence that proves that he was alive at least in the previous month. In either event we are informed that Edward Marshall was not present or the rest of the family injured. We must remember that when so many murders were committed that the circumstances became in time confounded with each other, hence the liability to such discrepancies unless immediately written down.

Sometime in the latter part of 1758, Edward Marshall was married to Elizabeth, the daughter of Nicholas Wiser, who was now in her thirtieth year. Her father was a native of Nieuwied on the Rhine and in 1748 he purchased by patent a tract of land containing 133 acres situated in Chestnut Hill township, about five miles north of the Wind Gap, on which he made the first improvements. As is not unusual with German immigrants, he appears to have flourished here until the beginning of the war, when he became one of its early victims. Mutual sympathy in part must have aided to draw Edward Marshall and his bride together. He had lost a wife and son and she had lost her father by the Indians, and also witnessed the destruction of his property by the devouring flames. This relationship induces us to give an account of the affair as taken down from her brother Leonard immediately on his return from captivity in the following summer.

His father resided on the north side of the Mountain and on the 31st of Dec., 1755, he was attacked by a body of thirty Indians, taking him and his brother William prisoners. After being pinioned they proceeded onwards until night. The next day they were left under the care of five Indians who went towards the Susquehanna, and the rest returned for further deeds of violence. After several weeks the other Indians returned with more captives, taken in the neighborhood where they had lived. They now all went up the river in canoes to Tioga and from thence up the Cayuga Branch about two hundred miles, where they lived in scattered parties. The prisoners were as well used as could be expected, living as the Indians did, only that they were obliged to do their servile work. Sometime in the spring while Tedyuscung was twenty miles above Tioga, two Mingo or Iroquois Indians came on a message from their nation, stating that if they did not desist from their hostilities against the English they would come and destroy them and all the Indians on the Susquehanna river. Owing to this circumstance he with his brother and two other captives were brought to Fort Allen and released through presents given to the captors.

On the following 17th of January, John Adam Huth, in company with several others, proceeded beyond the Blue Mountain, and when they came to the late residence of Nicholas Weiser all was found in ashes, and the cows, sheep and hogs lying dead around the place. Besides Mrs. Marshall and the two mentioned there were two more sons, Frederick and Nicholas. The latter afterwards moved to Montgomery county, New York, where he was still residing in 1792, when he sold the homestead to Jacob Stroud. Leonard Weiser, in 1761, resided in Lower Smithfield, and in the summer of 1763 joined Capt. John Van Campen's company

to resist further Indian incursions into Northampton
county. The effects of these ravages had been such
that on an enumeration made in 1758, there were ascertained to be only thirty-five horses and nine wagons
remaining in Mount Bethel township, the home of
Edward Marshall.

CHAPTER V.

BOUNTIES FOR DESTROYING INDIANS.

After these several attacks by the Indians on the family and relations of Edward Marshall, and perchance his own very fortunate escape therefrom, the question arises whether any efforts were made on his part to retaliate or resist their further incursions and ravages? On no subject connected with the life of this individual have we felt more disposed to exercise caution from the very nature of its seriousness. Back even into the days of our boyhood, and not many miles from his island home, we had heard of numerous traditions still lingering of the merciless revenge he sought and found in the wanton destruction of the savages. As years rolled on and we had attained manhood and the experience of an author, it gleamed on us that the biography of the hero of the famous Indian Walk was deserving a record. This now brought us more in contact with his numerous descendants. We were surprised in our inquiries that they seemed to have faith in the truth of the traditions that he had sought and found retaliation during the Indian war whilst a resident of Northampton county, or in New Jersey, opposite. From the excellent character that he, his brothers and the family always have borne among their neighbors and acquaintances, it is right that we should seek some palliation therefor in this chapter.

As far as Pennsylvania was concerned, the earliest information, or rather suggestion, on this matter that we have found, is in a letter from Edward Shippen, dated Lancaster, December 16, 1755, and addressed to Wm. Allen, Chief Justice of the Province: "There is one James Patterson," he writes, "who lives about fifty miles from Harris' on Juniata where he has built a stockade fort and has twenty men with him, which has been the only means of protecting the settlers and to keep them on their plantations. He is a courageous, resolute fellow and is resolved to stand his ground, if he can be encouraged with a few arms and some ammunition. He wants very much to know whether any handsome premiums is offered for scalps, because if there is he is sure his force will soon be augmented."

William Peters wrote from Philadelphia, January 4, 1756, to Thomas Penn, that it is "the wish of almost every body here that notwithstanding your most generous presents and the large sum granted for defending the country and driving off the Indians, little good will be done without giving handsome rewards for scalps. And to set the example a subscription has been handed about in the Coffee House to encourage the bringing in the heads of these two villains Shingas and Captain Jacobs. The two Delaware chiefs who have been so remarkably carressed by us are said to have the principal hand in drawing off the other Delawares and Shawanese. Seven hundred dollars were presently subscribed and this with the Governor's approbation published in our newspapers. The Governor and Commissioners being also convinced of its necessity, it is expected that as soon as they have settled with our friendly Indians, if any come to the treaty, the mode of doing it so that a proper distinction may be made between the enemy Indians and those who are or may be inclined to be our friends. The Governor will then immediately issue a Proclamation for offering proper rewards for Indian scalps." On the following 7th, he writes: "Since the encouragement proposed to be given for scalping and the Governor and Commissioner's tour amongst the people in the back counties, their spirits seem to revive, and several companies, chiefly composed of those who have been used to deer hunting and are good marksmen, have voluntarily offered themselves and some of them actually gone and others going against the Indians."

On the 12th of January, Dr. Franklin, as Colonel of a Pennsylvania regiment, issued an order to Capt. John Van Etten, of Upper Smithfield, Northampton county, wherein he says: "You are to acquaint the men that if in their ranging they meet with, or are at any time attacked by the enemy, and kill any of them, forty dollars will be allowed and paid by the government for each scalp of an Indian enemy so killed, the same being produced, properly attested." The Rev. Richard Peters, in a letter to Thomas Penn, dated Philadelphia, February 17th, uses this strong language: "The general voice of the people cries aloud for a Proclamation offering rewards for Indian scalps, and most are of opinion that this will effectually engage numbers to range and lie in the woods and surprise the Indians in the same manner that they do our miserable people."

"If I was so happy," writes Conrad Weiser, Feb. 28th, to Thomas Penn, "as to have two or three hours' conversation with you or with your Honor's brother, Mr. Richard Penn, I flatter myself several things in this Province would soon alter for the better, especially Indian affairs. I fear that rudeness, lawlessness and ignorance of the back inhabitants not only of this but also of the neighboring Provinces will bring a general Indian war over us. They curse and dam the Indians and call them murdering dogs into their faces without distinction, when on the other hand these poor Indians that are still our friends do not know where to go for safety; in the woods they are in danger of being killed, or their young men joining our enemy. Among us they are in danger of being killed by the mob, and what is pityful, we have little or no government within our doors."

Thomas Penn wrote in reply to William Peters, July 7th: "I wish," he says, "our people had been willing to join in companies to destroy them and bring in their wives and children, rather than money should be publicly offered for scalps, which is much disliked here, and in some of the French pieces lately published we are reproached with it as a cruel and unchristian-like practice. It certainly encourages base private murders and should therefore be practiced only in very particular cases, and I fear for the reward some people may trespass beyond their bounds." The same to Governor Hamilton, three days later: "When you wrote me last, you regretted you were not at liberty to declare war against the Delaware Indians, that you might attack them in their towns. This inconvenience is since removed, and I wish people enlisted in pay could have been found to go in small parties and attack them, making prisoners of their wives and children, as a means to oblige them to sue for peace, rather than rewards should be offered for scalps, especially of the women as it encourages private murder."

As may be supposed the result of this was a proclamation by Gov. Robert Hunter Morris at Philadelphia, April 14, 1756, from which we make this extract: "I have therefore by and with the advice and consent of the Council, thought fit to issue this Proclamation, and do hereby declare the said Delaware Indians and all others, who in conjunction with them have committed hostilities against his Majesty's subjects within this Province, to be enemies, rebels and traitors to his most sacred Majesty. And I do hereby require all his Majesty's subjects of this Province, and earnestly invite those of the neighboring Provinces to embrace all opportunities of pursuing, taking, killing and destroying the said Delaware, and all others confederated with them in committing hostilities, incursions, murders or ravages upon this Province." In consequence the following offers were made: for every male Indian enemy above twelve years old taken prisoner 150 Spanish dollars; for the scalp of every male Indian enemy above the foregoing age and killed 138 Spanish dollars; for every female Indian taken prisoner under the age of twelve 138 Spanish dollars, and the same for male; for the scalp of every Indian woman killed 50 Spanish dollars.

Richard Peters wrote to Thomas Penn, April 30th: "Two of the Six Nations and four or five of the friendly Delawares who went on Tuesday charged by the Governor with a message to the Susquehanna Indians to certify to them what had passed between Col. Johnson and the Deputy of the Six Nations, returned from Obsaningo, and that they might not fall in the way of our people who were extremely incensed and be exposed to the scalping parties that might go out in hopes of gain for scalps, the Indians were desired to advise the Susquehanna Indians to keep a distance and await the issue of the proposals that might be agreed to by Col. Johnson."

Notwithstanding a war of extermination had been carried on against the Indians for over eight and a half years, Gov. John Penn issued an additional proclamation, dated July 7, 1764, wherein he states that he does "declare the said Delaware and Shawanese Indians, and all others who in conjunction with them have committed hostilities, and I do hereby require all his Majesty's subjects of this Province, to embrace all opportunities of pursuing, taking, killing and destroying the same and all others concerned in committing hostilities, murders, or ravages upon this Province.

And whereas it is necessary, for the better carrying on to a close, that the greatest encouragement should be given to all his Majesty's subjects to exert their utmost endeavors to pursue, attack, take and destroy our said enemy Indians, that there shall be paid to all and every person and persons not in the pay of this Province, the following several and respective premiums and bounties: That is to say for every male prisoner above ten years old 150 Spanish dollars, for every female and male under age 130 Spanish dollars. For the scalp of every male above ten years 134 Spanish dollars and female 50 Spanish dollars, and to all those as soldiers in the pay of this Province half this sum. To be paid on the delivery at any Fort garrisoned by the troops in the pay of this Province, or at any of the county towns by the keepers of the Common Gaols."

He excepts from the foregoing the Six Nations and some Delawares and Nanticokes who live in friendship and under the protection of the Government. The Governor who had now increased the bounties for the destruction of Indians was the grandson of Wm. Penn and before the arrival of the latter the Swedes had lived with the Indians in harmony for forty years. But in justice to Mr. Penn our historians have generally overlooked the fact that his proclamation on the subject had been preceded by a former one. When this became known in France the press and general opinion there was strongly against carrying on so barbarous a system of warfare and which to their great credit was not permitted, but who turned it to greater account by additionally stimulating their allies to greater exertions in resisting the further aggressions of the English. Among those famed "for searching for and killing the Reds" in Northampton county, and no doubt incited thereto by the rewards and encouragements thus offered, may be mentioned George La Bar, Ulrich Hauser and Tom Caspar. It may be well asked what has become of those Indian scalps, and the documents and records connected with this business? No information on this subject has yet been elicited to our knowledge.

Edward Marshall is represented by his descendants as rather taciturn, or having very little to say respecting Indian exploits. One of the daughters of Martin Marshall informed us over thirty years ago that her father had said that on one occasion he had pressed him to relate his adventures with the Indians. After musing a few seconds, the only reply was, when he discovered an Indian he would shut one eye and they would not meet again. The stories generally circulated about him on these matters have been so extravagant that we have declined their use. However, we will briefly relate two of his adventures that under the circumstances seem plausible. While out hunting during the war he unexpectedly met an armed Indian within one hundred and fifty feet of him. Both immediately took to trees and kept manœuvering for each other's lives. After a long interval Marshall took off his hat, placed it on his ramrod and kept operating it now on one side the trunk of his tree and then the other. Soon a report followed and he dropped the hat to the ground. The Indian rushed forth with a yell, tomahawk in hand, for his scalp, but when within thirty feet he aimed, shot and killed him. On another occasion a somewhat similar occurrence happened. After being behind their respective trees for some interval, Marshall shouted out a proposal for relieving themselves; that instead they would shoot at some mark and offered to shoot first. The Indian approved it and arranged for the mark, which was to be about half way between them and some fifteen yards to one side. Marshall said he was ready but to prevent dispute must distinctly understand what mark. The Indian hereby lost his caution by projecting himself to indicate it when Marshall shot and he dropped to the ground.

CHAPTER VI.

RETURN TO BUCKS COUNTY.

In consequence of the several attacks made by the Indians on the family of Edward Marshall, and the distress and loss occasioned thereby, his brother William, of Tinicum, being in a languishing condition, and having no children, kindly remembered him in his will, made on the 18th of August, 1757, and but a few weeks before his death. He first requires therein that his wife Ann shall have the full use and benefit of all his estate for three years, and next states: "I give unto my beloved brother Edward Marshall after the term aforesaid all my estate, right, title and interest of, in and to my leased lands and the Island in the Delaware called Tinicum Island, together with all and every the buildings and improvements to the said Land and Island belonging. Provided, that my said brother pay to his four sons, Peter, William, Moses and Martin, the sum of Fifty pounds like money aforesaid and a piece as they come to the age of twenty-one years." It was thus through the gift and remembrance of a brother after his recent misfortune that Edward came in possession of his island home, and to be retained and occupied by him to the close of his life, or for nearly the third of a century.

Of Edward Marshall's return to Bucks county with his family we are not able to a certainty to fix the date. His granddaughter, Eliza Kean, informed us that his sons Peter and Thomas, the first children by his second wife, were born in Tinicum, which would fix the date about 1759. The latter, from a family record, was born January 19, 1761, and survived until 1831. Farming, with hunting and fishing, chiefly engrossed his attention. With the commencement of the Revolution he must have been aged about sixty years, and consequently no longer the hale and active or vigorous man of his prime. He heartily concurred in the Independence of his country, and we find that he gave in his allegiance before his neighbor, Nicholas Patterson, a Justice of the Peace, November 30, 1777, and his son Moses the following 21st of July. For the use of Washington's army, and to prevent their getting into the hands of the British, or assist their crossing into Pennsylvania, all the boats, flats and scows were collected up to his island. William and Moses, his eldest sons, went with their boats, which had also been pressed into the service, to render their aid in ferrying as well as securing all boats to the west bank of the Delaware until the danger of invasion from the Jersey side should be over. This was particularly the state of affairs towards the close 1776 and the beginning of 1777. Indeed the British had made a forced march in the night near the beginning of December to Coryell's Ferry with this particular object in view, but found themselves disappointed and marched back to Pennytown.

As published in Watson's Annals: "In the revolutionary war, the Indians again returned from west of the Ohio into Tinicum, still aiming at Marshall, and he again escaped by being from home; they then went back through Jersey." We made minute inquiries into this matter about forty years ago among some four or five of his grandchildren, who were born and resided all their days in that vicinity, as well as about a dozen of his later descendants, and they all emphatically deny this statement, that any efforts prompted by a spirit of revenge had ever been made with any hostile intent whilst he resided here. Had such an expedition been made it would have been doubtful if it would have arrived safely through so thickly a settled country.

Samuel Preston relates in a communication written in 1826, that in 1782 and the following year he had formed his first acquaintance with Edward Marshall. Having been called on as a surveyor to settle some old lines in Tinicum and Nockamixon townships he required his assistance to show him the boundaries. "To me," he says, "he appeared a respectable old man of good memory and fair standing as to veracity, in his testimony respecting lines and corners. He was a native of Bucks county, and a large, heavy-set, strong-boned man. He was then living on his large Island, had been a noted hunter and chain carrier for Nicholas Scull. He gave me a statement of his great Walk in which he was fully determined to beat or die in the attempt."

Almost to his last Edward Marshall retained his physical powers but little impaired by age. Laboring under the effects of a severe cold with a short attack of influenza brought about his death November 7, 1789, aged according to his own account seventy-four years. His granddaughter Eliza Kean informed us that his tombstone was not put up until about 1829 and that the inscription thereon was written by his son Thomas, one of the administrators, which makes him five years older, and in the absence of any written record he may have been led into error. He died on his Island and for greater convenience his body was conveyed to the house of his son Martin Marshall, living opposite on the river road and a few yards below the mouth of Tinicum creek, where the funeral was held, on which occasion the Rev. Nicholas Cox, a Baptist clergyman, delivered a discourse to a large assemblage. He was buried in the Marshall family burying ground, about one and a half miles distant. His grave at the present time is located a few yards west of its centre, over which a white marble stone is erected about three and a half feet high containing this inscription: "In memory of Edward Marshall, Sr., who died November 7th, 1789, aged 79 years.

> Unveil thy bosom faithful tomb
> And give these sacred relics room,
> Take this frail treasure to thy breast
> To slumber in thy silent dust."

The house in which the funeral was held is still standing, being a large substantial two-story stone edifice said to have been finished but a few days before this occasion, which its appearance would indicate. It has long been in possession of Sarah, wife of David Spear, who is a daughter of the said Martin Marshall, to which is attached a farm of fifty acres. She had previously been married to Samuel Weisel, deceased. This property she received by inheritance.

At his death Edward Marshall left fourteen surviving children, six sons and eight daughters, hence we need not wonder at his having numerous descendants. These were William, Moses, Martin, Catharine married to William Ridge, Elizabeth to Immanuel Pidcock, Jemima, deceased, to Nathan Allen, but leaving children, Naomi to William McCalla, Amy to Thomas Tillyer, Peter, Thomas, Edward, Mary, Anne, Sarah and Rebecca. Of these and their descendants we will have more to say hereafter. His estate was settled by Thomas Marshall and Thomas Tillyer and an appraisement made of his personal property by Nicholas Wyker and John Neis on the following 23d of December, amounting to £749, 1s, 9d. In this was embraced wearing apparel, cash and bonds £379, 18s, 10d; 300 bushels of corn in the ears and a mare and colt £82 ; wheat and rye and a field of grain £94, 13 cattle, 22 sheep, 13 hogs £44,9s ; wagon and gears, 3 cider barrels, cutting box, 4 spinning wheels, 6 bedsteads and bedding, carpenter tools, 2 guns, 2 plows, 1 boat, 2 canoes, a flat, etc. His real estate, besides the island of 128 acres and improvements, consisted of a plantation of 212 acres, which he had purchased May

8, 1787, of Rachel Stewart and son Robert, situated on both sides of Tinicum creek and approaching within less than a mile of the island and adjoining his other land on the south.

We estimate that the total value of Edward Marshall's real and personal estate at the time of his decease was very nearly $10,000, certainly a handsome sum for this period. With all his proclivities for hunting, gunning, fishing and adventure, he was yet so good a business manager, that from his first starting out for himself until the close of his life financial distress was a matter unknown to him. Hence we do not wonder at the independent spirit of his character. From the records of Northampton county we have ascertained that Elizabeth Marshall, the widow, was still residing in Tinicum township, February 6, 1792, when she conveyed for £100 all her right and title unto her brother Nicholas Weiser of Cherry Valley, New York, in the family homestead of 133 acres of land in Chestnut Hill township, which the latter sold a few weeks thereafter to Col. Jacob Stroud, of Stroudsburg. She afterwards removed to the residence of her daughter Rebecca, married to Neal Kean, a short distance below Frenchtown, where she died October 12, 1807, aged nearly 80 years. A stone with an inscription denotes her burial place beside the remains of her husband in the family graveyard.

William Marshall, the eldest brother of Edward, died in Tinicum, some time in September, 1757. In his will, dated the 18th of August previous, he leaves his wife Ann the full benefit of all his estate for three years, after which she is to have, in lieu of any dower, all his best furniture and table ware, the "Negro wench named Mooney," his mare and £200 in money. To his brother he leaves all his leased lands and the island in the Delaware river called Tinicum, with all the buildings and improvements thereon, providing that he pay to his sons Peter, William, Moses and Martin £50 apiece as they come to the age of twenty-one years; to his brother John Marshall £31, and his sister Rebecca's two sons Abraham and Benjamin Overfelt £20 each. His watch he leaves to his brother Moses, after which the residue shall be equally divided between his brother John and the aforesaid mentioned nephews. John Watson, the well-known surveyor of Buckingham, was appointed his executor. In the inventory of his effects as appraised by William Nash and John Russell we find mention made of "a negro man named Jim" valued at £35, the "molatto wench Mooney" £30, 16 head of cattle, 10 horses, 27 sheep, 27 swine, wagon, 3 guns, wolf trap, boat, 2 canoes and a flat; the whole of the personal amounting to £558, 5s, 6d. This would indicate for the times a productive farm of some size.

Moses Marshall, the second brother of Edward, is said to have been a gunsmith by occupation and that he followed this business to some extent in Tinicum. We infer that he died in 1773, for Sarah, his widow, it appears from a petition to the Court of Quarter Sessions for Northampton county, dated June 21, 1775, had moved up there, and which states that Jacob Wood, of Mount Bethel township, as administrator of her husband's estate, was required on account of an error of £84 to resettle the same. In the assessment of Tinicum township for 1779, we find his estate taxed for £71, 9s on 236 acres of land, 3 horses and 3 cattle, the business probably being carried on by Thomas Tillyer, "a single man," until at least to 1783. His son Jonas Marshall and wife Hannah had moved in 1775 to Surry county, North Carolina, and the following year sold their place of 15 acres and "the Moses Marshall Island" of 45 acres in the Delaware to William Ridge for £200. We thus perceive that the Marshalls were successful business men of property, quite so for the period, when we come to consider the limited means of so new a country.

CHAPTER VII.

FAMILY REMINISCENCES AND TRADITIONS.

Edward Marshall is represented as having been a tall, muscular and stoutly built man. He was at least six feet one inch in height, and by some he is mentioned as having been even two or three inches taller. He was never regarded as a fluent talker and had but little to say on the most familiar subjects. He retained to the close of his life a fondness for smoking the pipe. As a neighbor he was popular and we have not been enabled to learn of any reflections regarding his character. As respects the advantages of school learning they must have been limited. We cannot find that himself or his brothers or second wife and sons William and Moses could write their names, merely making their initials or marks therefor. They could read and make ordinary calculations and little more. We must remember that in a country so new and sparsely settled the means of acquiring an education was not very readily secured, yet we find through their good sense and native shrewdness that the Marshalls were good and successful business men, proving that they were possessed of no mean intellectual abilities however neglected in early life.

Concerning the reward that he may have received for performing the Walk much has been said and written of a contradictory nature. We have given this matter sufficient attention to form thereon an opinion. In the Penn Accounts for Indian charges under date of 3d of 7th-month, 1735, mention is made of having "Paid Timothy Smith for the three persons that walked out the Indian Purchase in Bucks county £15." This was for the Trial or Experimental Walk kept secret from the Indians and which would be £5 apiece. In the said charges for October 5, 1737, we find "To cash paid T. Smith for ye men who travelled ye Purchase £10, 3s, 9d." This would denote that it had been paid to Mr. Smith for the walkers about two weeks after the occurrence, with perhaps no allowance to Solomon Jennings for non-performance. Joseph Smith, of Tinicum, whose father was a nephew of the said sheriff Timothy Smith, stated, in a communication in 1826, that the aforesaid had in addition to the £5 offered a reward of 500 acres of land within said purchase to the one that should walk the furthest in eighteen hours. In the papers of the Friendly Association used at the Treaty at Easton in 1757, we find this information: "Marshall, on applying to the Proprietaries for a reward, was offered five pounds, which he rejected with contempt and has never had any reward." This corroborates exactly what has always been attributed to Marshall and confirmed by his descendants, of his refusing anything short of the reward that had been publicly offered and afterwards withheld by the Proprietaries. However, he lived to see them lose "Our Province of Pennsylvania," and the country and himself in the end were the better for it. Revolution with retribution had come and the Marshalls were forever rid of quit-rents or holding any longer leased lands.

In connection with the Walk there is a family tradition that Edward stated that when he had finished the one and a half day's Walk at the Five Chestnut Oaks with a hatchet he cut a small chip from out of one of those trees for identity and brought it away with him to retain in evidence should it be required in the future the distance he may have traveled.

Samuel Preston, in a letter to John F. Watson in 1828, states that Edward Marshall showed him a pocket compass which had been given to him to use through the woods near the termination of the Walk and his retaining it was all the compensation he had received for that undertaking. As his using a compass has been denied by the Proprietary party, we give from Timothy Smith's evidence this extract: "Kept on old Indian path till they came to a place called Pockopoghkunck; that from thence they proceeded through the woods by a compass which was carried by Benjamin Eastburn or Nicholas Scull and then stopped at the top of the mountain where they marked five chestnut oaks as the end of the said one and a half day's walk." Respecting it Edward Marshall says that from Pockopoghkunck continued the walk "through the woods north-northwest by a compass, which this affirmant carried in his hand, but had not used before, and pursuing that course or bearing hard all the time and the said Yates having given out and stayed at Tobyhanna creek, this affirmant continued the walk in company with Alexander Brown who carried the watch." Respecting this matter in the report by the Council they say "we examined particularly Marshall who says he carried a compass at the time, besides his being contradicted in that circumstance, we think it very improbable he should, as it must have retarded his walking if he stopped frequently to make any use of it, that he could not possibly walk so far in the eighteen hours as he says in his deposition." Here is an evident attempt at misconstruction, its use being only requisite near its termination when they had got beyond all the paths or routes that had been previously opened to travel over, and as the result indicates had extended further than those in the Proprietary interests had anticipated. On inquiry as to the whereabouts of this compass we were informed by Dr. James Ridge, of Camden, N. J., a great-grandson, that about forty-five years ago a member of the family had accidentally dropped it in crossing the Delaware and it was thus unfortunately lost.

His descendants relate that after his return to Tinicum he was in the practice late in the fall of going up in the Beech woods hunting, for weeks, when he would embrace the occasion to visit his numerous relatives there, as the Marshalls, Overfields, Weisers and others. Whilst up there on one occasion he observed across a valley a herd of seven deer; at the foremost, a noble buck, he aimed with his rifle. The bullet took effect at the root of the horn of a younger animal in the rear, who dropped to the ground. In arriving there the distance seemed so great that he concluded to satisfy himself by stepping it off, and made it a trifle over 400 yards or about a quarter of a mile. However, it must be remembered that this was over the surface of the ground, the valley intervening. His friends up there would relate of his saying on his return from hunting, that if they were short of venison to go to a certain place on a small tree or sapling, where a saddle would be suspended. It is said that numbers of poor families would go on such missions to their surprise at his suggestion. In one of these adventures he came to a bluff overlooking a deep narrow glen through which flowed a small stream. A slight noise there among the leaves attracted his attention, when to his surprise he observed it occasioned by a half grown panther, performing all the antics of a playful kitten. The longer he stayed there witnessing so singular a scene from its supposed savage nature the more its novelty impressed him. As a consequence he came away leaving it unharmed.

As Samuel Preston had stated that Edward Marshall had found a silver mine in the vicinity of his island and retained it a secret, we concluded to make some inquiry on the subject. His granddaughter, Mrs. Sarah Spear, informed us in May, 1873, that there had been such a report and its location placed along the hill sides of Tinicum creek and within less than a mile of its mouth. While having no knowledge of the tradition William Ridge stated that ore had been found there which on an analysis was found to contain silver. The existence of lead, silver and gold in this immediate vicinity has actually been mentioned by Lindstrom, the Royal Swedish engineer, and also by Robert Evelyn in 1648. The location was placed in "stony hills" along the Delaware about thirty miles above the first falls. It was prudent to keep such discoveries secret, for under the Colonial rule the charters required from all the workers thereof *three-fifths to the King and Proprietary*, and this excessive tax was styled by William Penn an "encouragement of such as are ingenious and willing to search out gold and silver mines in this Province."

In company with our antiquarian friends Joseph D. Armitage and Cyrus Livezy of Lumberville, we visited the Marshall graveyard September 24, 1871. It is situated on the south side of a hill about half a mile north of Tinicum creek, comprising a quarter of an acre enclosed by a substantial stone wall. The principal names on the stones containing the inscriptions are Marshall, Wood, Tillyer, Meyers, Ott and McIntyre. In the older portion a number of graves are denoted by common stones. Besides Edward Marshall and wife, some of his children, grandchildren and numerous relations repose here, of whom we shall have more to say. It is a family tradition that this site came to be selected under the following circumstances: That when two young women of the Marshall family were taking a stroll here, one of them expressed a wish that on her death she be buried at this spot as an appropriate place. Within a few weeks she was accidentally drowned and this proved in consequence the first corpse interred here. This must have occurred sometime before 1757, or more than a century and a quarter ago, and they may have been the daughters of William or Moses Marshall, brothers of Edward.

CHAPTER VIII.

MARSHALL'S ISLAND.

We know, from the will of Wm. Marshall, made in 1757, that the original name of this island was Tinecong or Tineconk, and that the stream emptying opposite as well as the township thus received the appellation. Its signification in the Delaware language was an island covered with woods, and has with time become changed into Tinicum. We have been unable in the records to trace back its earlier title, and, as has been stated, it came into the possession of Edward Marshall through his brother's legacy. The Commissioners of Pennsylvania and New Jersey, in 1786, confirmed to Tinicum township "Prall's two islands, Wall's island, Resolution island, Marshall's island, Wall's two islands, Fishing island and Pennington's island." On the large Township Map of Pennsylvania by Reading Howell, published in 1792, "Marshall's Island" is represented lying opposite the mouth of Tinicum creek, with a house on it a little north of its centre. A road is represented as coming from "Irwin's" above to Tinicum creek, thence turning southwestwards to the Durham road. This island is correctly represented thereon as situated almost in the middle of the Delaware.

We would infer from said will that there were buildings on this island in 1757, but whether Wm. Marshall resided thereon at that time we are unable to say. Edward Marshall is mentioned as having resided here in a large two-story log house, which, from the size of his family, and the amount of his household furniture and fixtures mentioned in the inventory, would be deemed necessary. It would appear that some time after the death of Edward Marshall, a division of a portion of his real estate was made among his heirs, and that this island came into the possession of his son Martin, whom we know died before 1821, and was sold by his heirs April 1, 1836, to Price Pursell, of Nockamixon township, for $2,942.85. By a survey then made it was found to contain eight perches less than one hundred and twenty-eight acres. About 1850 it was sold by John M. Pursell, trustee for Thomas Pursell, to Henry S. Stover, and by the latter, in 1858, to Hugh Capner, of Flemington, N. J., who deceased before 1873.

In company with Wm. Ridge, a great grandson of Edward Marshall, we visited this island May 18, 1873. It was one of those fine sunny spring days, tempered by a light breeze from the north. We crossed in a boat from Eichline's Hotel, which is nearly opposite its central part, and found by our journey there that the river was considerably wider than we had expected and possessed a strong current. At our landing we observed a very fine view looking north. The bridge at Frenchtown, spanning the Delaware two miles off, with the spires and houses of said place in sight, and beyond the long and high range of Musconetcong Hills towards the northeast at a distance of from fifteen to twenty miles, is still fresh in our recollection. Although Mr. Ridge did not reside three miles from here, he told us on this occasion that he had not been on this island before for twenty years. We first directed our steps to the house about forty yards from the landing, where we formed the acquaintance of the tenant, Howard Tettemer, who rented it on shares. Edward Marshall's house stood a few yards south of the present one, as did also his barn, from where it is now situated. A few old apple trees yet remained of its original orchard, five or six of which were now over two feet in diameter. The extreme length of the island is above one and quarter miles, and its greatest width about a fourth of a mile, and it is now assessed as containing one hundred and sixteen acres, of which twenty are still in woodland. It is undoubtedly the largest island in the Delaware within a distance of thirty miles, either above or below it. We should suppose that the house stands about eighteen feet above the surface of the river at its ordinary height. In the great freshet of 1841 three-fourths of the island was submerged with the water pretty near the buildings. Everything sent away or received here has to be ferried, for which purpose a scow or flat boat has to be kept. The tenant said the greatest objection he had to this was in transporting a loaded wagon with horses during high winds, which rendered it hazardous. The soil is sandy and does not appear to take well with grass.

In our strolls over its surface we were greatly impressed with the beauty of the surrounding scenery. The hills on the Pennsylvania and New Jersey sides generally rise into elevations of from thirty to one hundred and fifty feet above the Delaware. Tumble Falls is about a mile below, where rise perpendicular cliffs to upwards of one hundred feet in height, known as Warford's Rocks. The upper end of the island terminates in a point, where can be seen the effects of high floods in wearing away the soil. To our surprise on the shore here was lodged the trunk of a red maple over four feet in diameter and upwards of fifty feet in length that had been evidently brought hither from above during a freshet. Trees are still standing here of the original forest, consisting of chestnut, red and black oak, hickory, buttonwood, poplar, ash, paper birch, elm and linden. Some of these were above two feet in diameter. The whole island along its banks contains a fringe of trees about two rods in width, which is necessary for its protection from floods. Among these we observed several large and venerable chestnut trees. Both its upper and lower extremities indicate a considerable wearing away of its soil. Hence the importance of promoting the growth of trees. Among the most valuable for this purpose is the paper birch. The abundance of stone axes, pestles, spear heads and darts found would denote that here for a long period must have been a favorite abode or resort for the Indians. Otters abound but are now becoming rare.

One was captured here in 1842 by John Weisel, also a descendant of the family.

As we were about to leave the island on this our first and most probably last visit, a rush of recollections came thronging to us in connection with the long and last residence here of the famous pedestrian and hunter of whose like few examples can be found. On what his fame rests none now living can present experiences, for these have as irrecoverably gone as the time itself. We mean more particularly the Indians, the sway of the Penns, the deer, wolves and other game, and the associations connected therewith. In addition, we thought it was something to be brought here and have for our guide a descendant, a grandson too of his daughter Catharine,* who had so narrowly escaped a murderous assault from the savages. Now all was peaceful, and the bustling noise made on one side the river by the passing railroad train and the boatman's horn on the other betoken a change not known half a century ago; others even greater may soon follow. It is the duty of the historian or biographer to seize and collect these floating materials and prepare therefrom some memorials, that all is not lost. By such aids posterity will be the better enabled to judge and compare the past with times existing and the changes effected thereby.

---

*William Ridge died in Tinicum in 1886.

CHAPTER IX.

HIS DESCENDANTS.

William Marshall, the second son of Edward, was born in 1737, or the following year. For expressing himself against the conduct of the Penns in relation to the Indians he was informed against at Easton, a few weeks after the death of his mother, by Daniel Broadhead and Edward Biddle, though only about nineteen years of age, but with what result we are unable to state. He removed to Tinicum with his father and entered into farming. On the distribution of the proceeds arising from his father's personal estate in 1790, as the eldest surviving son under the existing law, he received a double share. With his brothers Martin and Edward the following year he purchased a farm of 100 acres for £300 from Col. George Wall, situated at the mouth of Tinicum creek, where they made their residence. Edward in 1800 sold his right in the farm for £170. William remained unmarried and made his home with Martin's family until in the spring of 1823, when he died, aged 85 years. His will bears the date of September 1, 1821; wherein he gives £100 and interest thereon to Buckingham Monthly Meeting "My rifle and shot gun with their accoutrements I give to William Marshall," the son of his brother

Moses. The balance of his estate he gives to his nieces, Rebecca, Sarah and Ann Marshall, the daughters of his brother Martin, deceased. He adhered to the principles of Friends, wore a plain coat and used their language.

Moses Marshall, the third son of Edward Marshall, was born in 1741. He was married to Agnes, daughter of Jacob Kulp, who had moved from Hilltown township to Tinicum in 1761, where he had purchased 212 acres from the London Company adjoining Edward Marshall's land. Moses in 1782 purchased a farm of 150 acres near the confluence of the North Branch with Pine run in New Britain township, where he resided until into the beginning of this century, when he sold it and purchased another of 158 acres near Mechanicsville, in Buckingham township, where he continued until his death, which took place June 22, 1828, aged nearly 88 years. His wife died only three months previously in her 87th year. Moses was sixteen years old when the Indians attacked the family of which he was a concealed spectator. He took the oath of allegiance in Tinicum, July 21, 1778, where he continued to reside until the spring of 1782. His will is dated Sept. 2, 1825, leaving to his sons William and Martin each a farm of 79 acres and a legacy to his daughter Mary. The sons afterwards sold their places and moved to Ohio and have descendants there. We were informed that the "rifle and shot gun with their accoutrements" were taken along and no doubt are still in possession of William's family.

We have supposed those to be the "two guns" mentioned in the inventory of Edward Marshall's effects, and if so the ones he may have frequently used.

Martin Marshall, the fourth son, in connection with his brothers William and Edward, purchased from Col. Wall a farm of 100 acres in Tinicum township opposite the Island in 1791, on which he continued to reside until his death, which we know was previous to 1821. He left four daughters, Sarah, Ann, Eliza and Rebecca. Catharine, the widow and the aforesaid heirs, sold the Island in 1836 to Price Pursell of Nockamixon for $2,942.85. Sarah was married to Samuel Weisel and after his decease to David Spear, became the owner of the homestead and 50 acres of land, on which she was still living in 1873, having been born here August 11, 1803. It was in this house where her grandfather's funeral was held in 1789, for which purpose his remains were brought from the Island, being on the way also to the family burying ground. Eliza was married to Thomas Pursell of Tinicum and Rebecca to Nelson Duckworth of Alexandria township, Hunterdon county. These three sisters were still living in 1873 at advanced ages. Ann was married to William McIntyre of Tinicum and we know she died before 1870. Nelson Duckworth and his family afterwards moved to the city of New York, having a son Morris who, we were informed, takes an interest in the family history. With the sisters Sarah, Eliza and Ann we were personally acquainted.

They furnished us interesting information for this work.

Of the seven sons of Edward Marshall but three were married; these were Moses, Martin and Peter. The latter was the first child by his second wife, having been born in 1759, and was called after his eldest son whom the Indians had killed in 1757. He moved from Tinicum to near Williamsport, Lycoming county, where he died July 25, 1806, aged 47 years, leaving also descendants. His son John died out there the latter part of December, 1871, aged about 80 years. Thomas, the sixth son of Edward, was born January 19, 1761, and survived until 1831. In connection with his brother-in-law Thomas Tillyer he settled his father's estate between December 1789 and April 5, 1792. In October 1791, he purchased his father's plantation of 212 acres on Tinicum creek, which he sold the following year to John Worman of said township. Edward Marshall, Jr., died February 4, 1802, aged 32 years, and with his brothers William, Martin and Thomas was buried in the family cemetery. Thomas T. Ridge informed us in 1873, that a tortoise had been found in the woods on the hill of that vicinity that had legibly cut on its under side the characters " E. M., 1792," evidently done by him in his 22d year.

Catharine, the eldest of Edward Marshall's daughters, was born about 1743, consequently when the attack was made by the Indians on the family in Northampton county she may have been aged 14 years. She was shot with a bullet through the body in escaping and concealed herself in a stream of water by which she staunched the flow of blood and eluded the vigilance of the savages who a few hours afterwards killed her mother. The wound occasioned the loss of her breast, but she reared twelve children, of whom eleven lived to be able-bodied men and women, two of whom attained to upwards of ninety years of age. William Ridge, her husband, was a carpenter by occupation and came from Bensalem before 1769. His father of the same name was a native of England and had settled in said township, where he died in 1776, aged 80 years, and his wife Mary survived until 1795, having attained the advanced age of 91 years. The son in 1775 purchased a farm of 79 acres of Robert Patterson, Esq., in Tinicum, for £240. The following year he purchased adjoining for £200, 15 acres with buildings and an island of 45 acres in the Delaware from Jonas Marshall (son of Moses) and his wife Hannah who had moved to Surry county, North Carolina. William Ridge died about 1821, aged 88 years. His children were Elizabeth, Thomas, William, Mary, Grace, Edward, Joseph, Catharine, Henry, Moses and Rebecca.

The present owners of the homestead are Thomas T. and Wm. A. Ridge, who are the twin sons of Moses, who died in 1860, aged 78 years. They informed us in 1873 that the island mentioned as containing forty-five acres, and so long known as Ridge's Island, had, through the action of the current, become reduced to a long, narrow gravel bar that at low water contained but three or four acres, on which now neither grass nor bushes grow. About forty years previously large trees were still flourishing on it, and it was then the resort of numerous birds. This purchase was originally made from John and Thomas Penn in 1769, and lay about half a mile below Marshall's Island. The aforesaid brothers are the present owners of a rifle that is said to have belonged to Edward Marshall, made at Rothenberg, Germany, and was purchased at the sale of Martin Marshall's effects. It is a flint-lock, and has the appearance of having seen considerable service though still in good order. The barrel is three feet one and a half inches in length, and the bore five-eighths of an inch in diameter with six grooves. Its total weight is nine and three-fourths pounds, and carries an ounce ball, which is sufficiently large to prove destructive. Dr. James Ridge, of Camden, N. J., is also a brother, as was Edward, lately deceased in Tinicum. Wm. Ridge, our guide to the island, is the son of Joseph, who has also furnished us interesting information respecting the Marshall family, as well as his cousins, with whom we have had an acquaintance for over forty years.

Elizabeth, the second daughter of Edward Marshall, was married before his decease to Immanuel Pidcock, and Naomi to William McCalla. Near the beginning of this century both moved, with Peter Marshall, their brother, to Williamsport, Lycoming county, where they have also descendants. Jemima, who was married to William Allen, died before her father and left several children. Amy married Thomas Tillyer, who, in a list of taxables for Tinicum, is mentioned in 1779 as "a single man living with Moses Marshall." He was married before 1789, and himself and wife were buried in the Marshall graveyard. The four remaining daughters, Mary, Ann, Sarah and Rebecca, were single in 1791. Mary married John Long and died in Philadelphia, August 26, 1829. Ann married Joseph Hinkle and died March 26, 1837, aged 72 years. Sarah died March 3, 1793, aged 25 years, and is buried in the family graveyard. Rebecca, the youngest, married Niel. Kean, and died at an advanced age near Frenchtown, N. J. A daughter Eliza was still living at the latter place in 1873, to whom we are also indebted for considerable information. She was the possessor of her grandfather Marshall's high-case eight-day clock and a chest of drawers that had been brought from England. The Hinkles are an old family in Plumstead and Tinicum. Philip Hinkle, the father of Joseph and Caspar, of Hinkletown, was a blacksmith in the Revolutionary army and cried the sale of Edward Marshall's personal effects in 1790. Dr. A. G. B. Hinkle, Rachel W., wife of Prof. J. W. Shoemaker, now of Philadelphia, and Mrs. Mary Wyker, of Tinicum, are from whom we have also received information, the children of William Hinkle, son of Joseph.

From what has been stated it will be observed that the descendants of Edward Marshall at this day must be numerous in Pennsylvania, New Jersey and Ohio. Although they have lived and flourished so long in

Bucks county and in the name are extinct, yet his descendants can there be numbered now by hundreds through intermarriage into families bearing the names of Ridge, Crout, Weisel, Hinkle, Meyers, Wyker, Weidenmeyer, Bergstresser, Pursell, Morehead, McIntyre, Buck, Nace and others. We have thought if his several thousand descendants, now so widely scattered over the Union, could read this imperfect and hastily prepared sketch, what an additional interest it would awaken, not only as to their family history, but of the hero of the famous Walk, with his extraordinary adventures and trials, that have been the subject hitherto of so many lingering traditions, and of the most vague and contradictory statements.

THE END.

INDEX.

Acrellus on Thomas Penn 162
Address to Gov. Denny 143, 146
Agent to reside in England 8
Allen, Wm., land dealings, 41, 42, 44, 45, 62, 163; character, 42, 47, 49; at Indian treaty, 66; biographical sketch, 163; importunate for office, 165; on Nutimus, 198; on Tedyuscung 80
Andros, Gov., purchase 25
Attack on the Weisers 227, 228
Appointing powers of the Penns..10, 13
Assembly, Governor's salaries, 9; committee from, 134; limited powers. 10; and the proprietaries, 24, 31, 39, 52, 77
Beale, Geo., requires a clear deed, 29
Beaver skin tribute 8
Biles, Wm., deposition 64
Bounties for destroying Indians 230
Bounds of the Indian purchase 49, 71
Broadhead and Biddle's charge 219
Brown, Alex., testimony, 61, 123, 172, 202, 213
Bucksville on line of Walk 102
Canassatego's speech, 50, 102, 109, 130, 193, 199, 210
Chapman, John, surveyor, 55, 60, 63, 81, 87, 102, 109, 110, 130; purchase, 27, 101; memoranda, 103; biographical sketch 181
Character of proprietaries 18
Charters set aside by Penn 12
Civility, a Delaware chief 40
Cobus creek 216, 225
Colonial Records and Archives 10
Combush and Joe Tuneam 87, 92, 95
Commissioners of property 38
Conference at Easton 121
Council, powers of, 10, 14; report from 146
Courts of Inquiry established 25
Court at Newtown 85, 211
Day, Sherman, on misgovernment, 17
Deed to Lehigh Hills, 65; authorizing the Walk 70
Delaware Indians, complimented, 21; to Judge Langhorne 49
Denny, Gov., and the Council, 122, 127, 215; reply to Friends, 149; examines Marshall 218
Depue, Nicholas, purchase 43

Difficulties of Colonial governors 9
Dingman, Andrew, purchase 45
Doane, Joseph 57, 58, 87, 210
Documents on the Walk 121
Du Ponceau on Penn's purchases 31
Durham purchase, 51; iron works, 89; road, 89, 93, 102, 208, 212; treaty, 76, 195
Dutch, Swedish and English purchases 25
Eastburn, Benj., map, 26, 97, 103, 104, 105, 119, 128, 130, 164; surveyor general, 45, 47, 95, 96, 101, 107, 119, 213; biographical sketch 167
Elective council abolished by Penn. 14
Expenses of the Walk 59, 106
Families related to the Marshalls...265
Feeling against the Penns 18
Felons, importation forced 12
Fendal prerogatives of the Penns..... 17
Franklin, Benj., agent, 16, 121; commissioner, 15; on the Penns, 19; on Thomas Penn, 159; orders on scalping 232
French opposed to scalping 236
Friendly Association, 54, 136, 139, 143, 146, 248
Forgery, charge of, 74, 75, 125, 130, 146, 215
Furniss, Thos., testimony, 84, 91, 94, 97, 100
Gallows Hill 89, 93, 212
Gallows erected for Thos. Penn 162
Gnadenhütten massacre 222
Goodwin, Ephraim, testimony, 60, 91, 94, 123, 196
Gordon's view of the Walk 114, 199
Governor's bonds 9
Great Shawnee Island 13
Hamilton's, Andrew, draft 64, 79
Harrison, Captain 87, 96
Heckewelder on Indian purchases, 45; on Indian names 197, 202
Heider, John, testimony, 63, 81, 91, 93, 104, 123, 179, 188
Hinkle, family account of 265
Hinkletown 208
Henry's History of Lehigh Valley, 116
Hockley's letters to Thos. Penn, 132, 145
Hockyondocqua, Indian town, 95, 97, 196, 201, 212

INDEX.

Holme's map of original surveys, 26, 100
Hughes, Mathew, at Marshall's 225
Indians, account of Walk, 91; attack on Marshall's family, 222, 226; dissatisfied, 27, 28, 31, 37, 41, 48, 50; 97, 113, 114, 116, 125, 172, 199, 201, 206, 214; danger of mobs, 233; desire to treat for lands, 32; defended by Logan, 37; kindness from, 21, 25, 189; murders in Northampton county, 222; furnished with books, 20, 21; purchases from, 23, 70; meeting at Durham, 54, 56, 67; portraits taken, 196, 197, 201, 202; dangerous to take their part, 199; their reservations not respected, 200; titles from, 23; language spoken with Hollanders, 173; treaty at Pennsbury, 57; war and the Walk, 15; threats............50, 199
Iroquois or Six Nations, 80, 115, 118, 193, 199
Jenks, Hon. Michael H............63, 102
Jennings, Solomon, notice of, 78, 83, 86; biographical sketch..............187
Johnson, Sir Wm., at Easton........31, 33
Judges, subserviency of................11
Kindness of Delaware Indians.........21
Kittatinny or Blue Mountains......49, 62
Knowles, Joseph......................61, 91
La Bar's reminiscences................113
Lands sold not granted by the Indians..................................36
Langhorne, Judge, and the Penns....120
Lawsuits of the Penns..............11, 29
Lappawinzo, notice of, 62, 95, 98; biographical sketch..................200
Lehigh river called Tobyhanna, 185, 213; hills of..........................191
Le Tort Indian trader.................202
Logan, James, purchases, 38, 39, 40, 206, desires Indian purchases, 33, 37; conduct as commissioner, 34; on Nutimus, 198; on Indian honesty.............................197, 202
Logan, William, 40, 107, 108, 123, 131, 134
Lukens, John, succeeds N. Scull....175
Luther's catechism in Indian..........20
Loudoun, Lord, conduct...............219
Markham's purchase................26, 64
Manawkyhickon's speech...........69, 72
Manor of Chawton.....................48
Marshall, Edward, mention of, 83, 86, 92, 94, 95, 98, 100, 105, 201; life of, 203; his brothers, 205; purchase, 205; removes to Northampton county, 216; wife killed, 225; son Peter killed, 226; his account of the Walk, 209, 211; encounter with Indians, 237; returns to Bucks county, 234; death and funeral, 242; personal and real estate, 244; his widow's death, 244; his descendants, 243, 259; reminiscences and traditions, 247; his island residence................................256
Marshall, Catharine, wounded........225
Marshall, John........................205
Marshall, Martin......................261

Marshall, Moses, on reward, 82; statement, 116, 117; notice of, 205; estate...............................246
Marshall Wm., notice of, 205, 207; will and estate, 239, 241; informed against.............................259
Marshall's creek......................218
Marshall graveyard...............205, 252
Minisink settlement, 42, 44, 113, 116, 118, 194
Minisink visited by Scull and Chapman.................................183
Misconduct of the Penns..............91
Morris, Gov., proclamation...........234
Mount Bethel township...........216, 229
Mysteries of the Walk........51, 76, 79
Names of persons at the Walk....91, 92
Northampton county, early account of..............................217
Nutimus notices of, 50, 62, 108, 115, 119; biographical sketch..............198
Observations on the Walk..............99
Opekasset and Shackalawlin..........192
Opposition to Indian rights, 22; to the proprietaries................12, 16, 18
Overfield, Abner and Benjamin, 216; Elizabeth, 205; family account of..............................220
Page, John, refuses unpaid grants...47
Peace was Penn's policy...............21
Pemberton, Israel, views on..........145
Penn Accounts, 55, 106, 170, 186, 192, 194, 196
Penn, John, at Durham, 54; Governor's marriage...................166
Penn, Richard, character, 18; son of William..............................53
Penn, Thomas, promises honesty, 33; extensive grant to Allen, 46; his character, 18, 51, 53, 86, 99, 152, 154, 155, 162; admits of discontent, 8, 120; address from the Assembly, 52; at Durham, 54; gives instructions on the Walk, 60; treats for the Walking purchase, 66; on the Walk, 75, 79, 83, 106, 108, 109; particular request, 85; opinion of Wm. Logan, 134; biographical sketch, 151; arrives with a Friends' certificate, 145; tries a scheme to get Franklin Square, 159; ill treatment of his nephew, 155; gets wounded and marriage, 154; opinion of the Quakers, 114; death, 161; gallows erected for him, 162; views on Eastburn's map, 168; considers Eastburn not honest, 171; tries to cheat his nephew William out of land.........155
Penn, Springett, and his guardian...155
Penn, William, code of laws, 9; correspondence with Logan, 25; to give clear Indian title, 29; required to civilize the Indians, 7, 30; justice, 67; commissioners of property, 38; family extinct in name, 112; death of.................53
Penn, Wm. Jr., receives a grant......42
Penns refuse to be taxed, 15, 16; generosity to, 161; query about........161

INDEX.

Pennsbury treaty..................67, 195, 200
Pennsylvania liberality....................161
Peters, Richard, on the Walk, 120;
  on the Quakers, 140; reply to, 140;
  reply to Assembly, 136; letters to
  Thos. Penn......140, 141, 176, 180, 232, 235
Peters, Wm., report on the Walk,
  125; letter to Thos. Penn............231
Petition to make Indian purchases. 32
Pocono mountain........................96, 213
Pokopoghcunk, an Indian settlement...........................96, 212
Power of the Penns, 10, 13, 14, 16, 24;
  of the Royal government............ 12
Preston, Samuel, on the Walk, 114;
  visits Marshall, 241; pocket compass..249
Proprietaries, government, 7; to
  pay tribute, 8; stipulations, 23;
  and Society of Friends.................137
Proclamations for destroying Indians...................................233, 235
Quakers, errors respecting, 137, 140,
  148, 150; benevolence of, 138, 139,
  223; charge against.............142, 145, 147
Records mystified............................ 49
Report of Council..........125, 127, 129, 131
Reservation by the Indians...........81, 200
Rewards for destroying Indians.......232
Reward for the Walkers.....82, 83, 86, 248
Ridge family, account of................263
Ridge, Wm., guide to Marshall's
  Island.....................................255, 258
Rights of the Indians...........20, 34, 206
Ronds, early, to Tinicum.................207
Royal charter to Penn, 7; proclamation... 35
Sassoonan and James Logan, 32, 37,
  65, 80; biographical sketch of........191
Scenery at Marshall's Island............255
Scull, Nicholas, 47, 91, 93, 95, 96, 104,
  123, 213, 217; biographical sketch,
  172; deposition on the Walk, 173;
  interpreter..................................104
Servility to the Penns..................... 18
Shackalimy, 80; biographical
  sketch of....................................193
Shippen, Edward, letter..................231
Sheriffs and Coroners, election of..... 13
Smith, Dr. Chas. W.........63, 101, 102, 118
Smith, Joseph........................63, 101, 104
Smith, Timothy, sheriff, 55, 57, 59,
  60, 63, 78, 83, 85, 88, 92, 95, 102, 109, 123,
  128; biographical sketch, 177; deposition on the Walk..................178
Starting place for Walk 26
Steel, James, letter, 57, 62, 85, 97, 109, 210
Streiper's purchase................28, 49, 206
Stokes' Meadow............................. 57

Society of Friends 110, 138, 148
Swedes, kindness to the Indians, 20;
  arrival 64
Swedish and German missionaries, 21
Tademi murdered.......................... 46
Taylor, Jacob, surveyor................... 41
Tedyuscung's charge, 100, 121, 129,
  131, 146, 147; and the Friendly Association..................................143
Termination of Walk.....................90, 95
Thomas, Governor..........................193
Tinicum township 207
Tishcohan, 62, 72, 98; biographical
  sketch 195
Tobyhanna creek.....................213, 250
Tohickon creek...............93, 195, 198, 205
Toleration in Rhode Island and
  Maryland 9
Trego, C. B., on the Walk................116
Trial Walk.......................53, 110, 180, 181
Triumph of Franklin's party........... 16
True and absolute Proprietary......... 15
Van Etten, Capt. John, 232; journal
  of..225
Vaux, Robert, on Thos. Penn.......... 51
Voltaire on the Great Treaty........... 30
Walking purchase.............65, 195, 201, 210
Walking, rapid..............................111
Walk, beginning and end of, 100, 165,
  212; distance of, 56, 104, 105, 109, 110,
  168, 174, 211, 214; expenses of, 55,
  59, 106; errors on, 110; depositions,
  123, 211; inquiry concerning, 121,
  123; postponed, 210; route of, 102;
  results of, 113, 117, 118; Marshall's
  account.......................................200
War of extermination waged.....233, 235
Warner, Thomas........................63, 102
Warrant of arrest for Thos. Penn....143
Warford's Rocks............................257
Watson, John Jr., account of Walk,
  115, 219
Watson, John, surveyor, 55, 63, 103,
  115, 207, 245
Watson, John F., on grants, 77; in
  error about Marshall....................241
Weiser, Conrad..........191, 193, 194, 233
Weiser, Nicholas, killed..................227
Whitefield's purchase from Allen... 45
Wiggins, Benjamin......................63, 102
Wilson, George, of Durham........93, 212
Witnesses on the Walk...................123
Wood, Dr., on Thos. Penn...............158
Wood's, John, land 65
Yates, James, 78, 83, 86, 93, 94, 96, 104,
  110, 168, 213; biographical sketch of..184
Zeisberger, David, missionary....21, 230
Zinzendorf, Count........................... 10

www.ingramcontent.com/pod-product-compliance
Lightning Source LLC
Chambersburg PA
CBHW031956230426
43672CB00010B/2178